KT-599-266

GOOD & HOUSEKEEPING
SLIM & HEALTHY
MICROWAVE COOKERY

GOOD & HOUSEKEEPING
SLIM&HEALTHY
MICROWAVE COOKERY

EBURY PRESS LONDON

Published by Ebury Press
Division of The National Magazine Company Limited
Colquhoun House
27-37 Broadwick Street
London W1V 1FR

First Impression 1987

ISBN 0 85223 645 X (Hardback)
0 85223 640 9 (Paperback)

Text copyright © 1987 by The National Magazine Company Limited
Illustrations copyright © 1987 by The National Magazine Company Limited

All rights reserved. No part of this publication may be reproduced, stored in a retrieval
system, or transmitted in any form or by any means, electronic, mechanical, photocopying,
recording, or otherwise, without the prior permission of the copyright owner.

The expression GOOD HOUSEKEEPING as used in the title of this book is the trade
mark of The National Magazine Company Limited and The Hearst Corporation, registered
in the United Kingdom and the USA, and other principal countries in the world, and is the
absolute property of The National Magazine Company Limited and The Hearst
Corporation. The use of this trade mark other than with the express permission of The
National Magazine Company Limited or The Hearst Corporation is strictly prohibited.

Senior Editor: *Fiona MacIntyre*
Editor: *Barbara Croxford*
Designer: *Bob Hook*
Photography: *James Murphy*
Stylist: *Cathy Sinker*
Cookery: *Janet Smith* and *Susanna Tee*
Illustrations: *Angela Barnes*
Cover photograph: Coriander chicken with mango sauce (page 93)

Filmset in Great Britain by Advanced Filmsetters (Glasgow) Ltd
Printed in Great Britain at The University Press, Cambridge

Contents

A NOTE TO
COMBINED COOKER
OWNERS

Combined cookers combine conventional and microwave methods of cooking so that food browns as well as cooking quickly. If you own a combined cooker you should follow your manufacturer's instructions on the technique of browning or crisping a dish. A disadvantage of cooking in a microwave cooker is that baked dishes do not brown or crisp. In this book, we show you how to overcome this disadvantage. However, if you own a combined cooker you will not have these problems. In this case, you should follow your manufacturers' instructions.

GENERAL RECIPE NOTES

Follow either metric or imperial measures for the recipes in this book; they are not interchangeable.

BOWL SIZES

Small bowl = about 900 ml (1½ pints)
Medium bowl = about 2.3 litres (4 pints)
Large bowl = about 3.4 litres (6 pints)

COVERING

Cook, uncovered, unless otherwise stated. *At the time of going to press, it has been recommended by the Ministry of Agriculture, Fisheries and Food that the use of cling film should be avoided in microwave cooking. When a recipe requires you to cover the container, either cover with a lid or a plate, leaving a gap to let steam escape.*

UNDERSTANDING POWER OUTPUT AND COOKER SETTINGS

Unlike conventional ovens, the power output and heat controls on various microwave cookers do not follow a standard formula. When manufacturers refer to a 700-watt cooker, they are referring to the cooker's POWER OUTPUT; its INPUT, which is indicated on the back of the cooker, is double that figure. The higher the wattage of a cooker, the faster the rate of cooking, thus food cooked at 700 watts on full power cooks in half the time of food cooked at 350 watts. That said, the actual cooking performance of one 700-watt cooker may vary slightly from another with the same wattage because factors such as cooker cavity size affect cooking performance. The vast majority of microwave cookers sold today are either 600, 650 or 700 watt cookers, but there are many cookers still in use which may be 400 and 500 watts.

In this book
HIGH refers to 100% full power output of 600–700 watts.
MEDIUM refers to 60% of full power.
LOW is 35% of full power.

Whatever the wattage of your cooker, the HIGH/FULL setting will always be 100% of the cooker's output. Thus your highest setting will correspond to HIGH.

However, the MEDIUM and LOW settings used in this book may not be equivalent to the MEDIUM and LOW settings marked on your cooker. As these settings vary according to power input we have included the following calculation so you can estimate the correct setting for your cooker. This simple calculation should be done before you use the recipes for the first time, to ensure successful results. Multiply the percentage power required by the total number of settings on your cooker and divide by 100. To work out what setting MEDIUM and LOW correspond to on your cooker, follow the same guidelines i.e.

MEDIUM (60%)

$$= \frac{\% \text{ Power}}{\text{required}} \times \frac{\text{Total number}}{\text{of cooker settings}} \div 100$$

$$= \text{Correct setting}$$

$$= \frac{60 \times 9}{100} = 5$$

LOW (35%)

$$= \frac{\% \text{ Power}}{\text{required}} \times \frac{\text{Total number}}{\text{of cooker settings}} \div 100$$

$$= \text{Correct setting}$$

$$= \frac{35 \times 9}{100} = 3$$

If your cooker power output is lower than 650 watts, then you must allow a longer cooking and thawing time for all recipes and charts in this book.

Add approximately 10–15 seconds per minute for a 600 watt cooker, and 15–20 seconds per minute for a 500 watt cooker.

No matter what the wattage of your cooker is, you should always check food before the end of cooking time to ensure that it does not get overcooked. Don't forget to allow for standing time.

HEALTHY EATING BASICS

Healthy eating is here to stay—experts agree more than ever about the changes that could improve our diet and help keep us in good health. Most people now know it means eating less fat—particularly saturated fat—sugar and salt and more fibre, but with the enormous choice of foods available the problem is knowing exactly what we should be eating. Adopting good eating habits usually means making changes but it doesn't mean sticking to a rigid diet or banning some foods altogether. It is simply a case of eating more of some foods and less of others, and thinking about how you prepare and cook foods—which is where the microwave comes in.

Microwaving is fast, clean and efficient; it can also help you get the best out of healthy ingredients. Foods cooked by microwaves retain their natural flavour, colour and texture and most cook in their own juices without the addition of fat or salt. The rapid cooking times also mean that nutrient losses are small compared to conventional cooking, even fast foods take on a healthy new meaning.

EAT LESS FAT

Some fat is essential in our diet—it supplies fat-soluble vitamins and certain types are vital for growth and development—but too much can be unhealthy. One of the reasons is that fat is very high in calories which can contribute to weight problems. Another is that diets high in fat are associated with serious diseases like coronary heart disease and breast and bowel cancer.

Fats can be divided into three basic types—saturated, monounsaturated and polyunsaturated. Too much saturated fat in particular is associated with increased risk of heart disease. Saturated fat tends to increase the amount of cholesterol in the blood which leads to the build-up of sludgy deposits on artery walls resulting in the blockages responsible for heart attacks and strokes. Monounsaturated fats (found in foods like avocado pears, nuts and olive oil) appear to have no effect on blood cholesterol levels; polyunsaturated fats may actually help to lower it.

It is advisable to eat less of all fats but especially saturated fat. A small proportion of the cholesterol in the blood comes directly from food so it is also a good idea to eat fewer concentrated sources of cholesterol like egg yolks.

How to cut down on fat
*Eat less fatty meats like pork, lamb and beef, and meat products such as pies, pasties, sausages, pâtés, cooked and cured meats. When you do use meat, choose lean cuts and trim off the visible fat. Serve with vegetables and pulses to make a smaller amount of meat go further.

Switch to poultry, rabbit, game and offal.

*Eat more fish—white fish are low in all fats; the polyunsaturated fat in oily fish may actually protect against heart disease.

*Eat fewer full-fat dairy foods such as whole milk, cheese, cream and ice cream. Switch to low-fat alternatives like skimmed or semi-skimmed milk, low- and medium-fat cheeses (Quark and Edam for instance) and yogurt.

*Avoid butter, block margarine, suet, lard and other shortenings. Choose polyunsaturated margarines, pure vegetable oils and low-fat spreads but limit the use of these, too.

*Buy less manufactured cakes, biscuits, pastries, crisps and other savoury snacks which often contain a lot of hidden fat.

*Use fresh herbs to flavour salads instead of fatty dressings like mayonnaise.

*Limit egg yolks to about six a week, including those in made-up dishes.

Fat and microwave cooking
Your microwave cooker can help in a healthy diet by cooking foods without additional fat but with no loss of flavour or succulence. Lean, tender cuts of meat are particularly suited to microwave cooking and are the best choice for healthy eating. Use a microwave roasting rack for fattier meats like chops and roasts—the fat drips away and can be discarded. Absorbent kitchen paper placed over bacon during cooking will also mop up surplus fat.

EAT MORE FIBRE

Fibre plays a vital role in keeping our bodies healthy. A mixture of different substances, most of it passes through the body unchanged. It may seem surprising that something with no nutritional value can be so important, but as well as preventing constipation, fibre appears to protect against diseases of the intestine like diverticulosis and bowel cancer.

Fibre works by holding a lot of water, making it easy for the intestine to push along the soft, bulky waste matter without pressure or straining. Potentially harmful substances are also diluted and got rid of quickly in this way. The fibre in cereals is especially good at absorbing moisture but other types play different roles in preventing disease; therefore, it is best to eat fibre from a variety of sources.

How to eat more fibre

Although there is no recommended intake for fibre, around 25 g (1 oz) a day is a healthy amount to aim for. Increasing fibre doesn't mean adding bran to everything; it is far better to eat foods that are naturally high in fibre. These include wholemeal bread, wholegrain breakfast cereals, brown rice and pasta, pulses, nuts, fruit and vegetables. Starchy, fibre-rich foods like bread and potatoes are not fattening when eaten in moderation and are a useful daily source.

Fibre and microwave cooking

There is no need to pre-soak fibre-rich dried fruits when cooking them in the microwave cooker, and they will be cooked in a fraction of the usual time. Although rice and pasta take just as long to cook, there is little chance of them sticking or boiling over and they can be reheated quickly.

EAT LESS SUGAR

Sugar is the carbohydrate we should all cut down on. It is high in calories but contains few nutrients. All sugar is damaging to teeth particularly when it comes in sticky forms like cakes, biscuits and sweets. The more often sugar is eaten the more harm it does—frequent sugary snacks are worse than the same amount of sugar in one meal. It is also thought that the sudden surges in blood sugar levels caused by regular sugary snacks can put a strain on the pancreas and increase the likelihood of developing diabetes later in life.

How to cut down on sugar

*Add less sugar to foods and drinks (this includes brown sugar, honey and syrups).

*Eat fewer sugary snacks like cakes, biscuits, sweets and soft drinks.

*Choose fruit, vegetables and salad as snacks instead.

*Switch to low or reduced sugar jams and preserves, low-calorie soft drinks and pure fruit juices.

*Check ingredient lists for glucose, dextrose, fructose, syrups and honey which are examples of hidden sugar—even foods labelled 'sugar-free' may contain them.

Sugar and microwave cooking

Use your microwave to help you cut down on sugar. Fresh fruits keep their appealing shapes and because they are full of natural flavour and sweetness there is no need to add sugar. Healthy alternatives to sugary snacks can be ready in minutes which makes it easier to avoid filling up on biscuits and other sugary snacks. You can still enjoy puddings, desserts and teatime treats by using the microwave cooker to make low sugar, nourishing alternatives, including the recipes in this book which are based on fresh or dried fruits for natural sweetness.

EAT LESS SALT

Salt is a compound of sodium and chloride but while both are essential in the body, it is believed that too much salt could have important implications for health. The theory is that an excessive intake of sodium leads to high blood pressure (hypertension) in susceptible individuals. Hypertension itself is a major risk factor in the development of heart and blood vessel disease, and it increases the risk of a heart attack or stroke. While there is still considerable disagreement about the effects of too much salt, many experts believe the evidence is sufficient to recommend that we all reduce our salt intake—it certainly won't do us any harm and may be beneficial for some people. What other experts think might be more important in the development of hypertension is the ratio of sodium to potassium in the body. They recommend that as well as cutting down as much as possible on sodium that it is also important to eat plenty of foods rich in potassium, including fresh fruit and vegetables.

How to cut down on salt
About one third of the salt we eat is added to food during cooking or at the table; the rest is already present in foods and most of that is added during manufacture. You can reduce the amount of salt in your diet by adding less to foods (sea and rock salt are no healthier than ordinary table salt) and eating fewer salty foods like preserved meats and meat products, smoked and salted foods, canned vegetables (salt-free versions are available, but pricey) and salted savoury snacks like nuts and crisps. Watch out for other forms of sodium like monosodium glutamate, baking powder and polyphosphates and go steady on salty ingredients such as soy sauce and stock made from cubes. Salt substitutes help some people wean themselves off the salt pot but they are expensive, often bitter tasting and some contain as much as 50% ordinary salt. They are unsuitable for people on potassium-restricted diets, and certain medical conditions.

Salt and microwave cooking

Food cooked in the microwave retains its flavour and needs little or no salt added. The rapid cooking times for fresh vegetables make it less tempting to reach for salt-containing canned and processed ones. Herbs can be used to add flavour instead of salt. (The microwave is ideal for drying fresh herbs since they retain their colour and strength of flavour.) Some of the recipes in this book include salt for seasoning; the use of salt is entirely optional and once you get used to less salty foods it can be left out altogether. There is no need to add extra salt to recipes containing ingredients like smoked fish or soy sauce, they will taste salty enough without any addition. Some commercially produced browning agents are very salty—use toasted seeds, chopped browned nuts or wholemeal breadcrumbs for healthier coatings and toppings instead.

VITAMINS AND OTHER NUTRIENTS

Eating a wide variety of healthy foods should ensure your body gets all the vitamins, protein and other nutrients it needs. Unhealthy eating habits could, however, mean you are going short of certain vitamins and minerals. Although vitamin supplements are unlikely to do any harm, they are not the best answer to poor eating habits. Use the chart to find out the best sources of vitamins, particularly those you think you might be lacking. If you still decide to take supplements, a daily multivitamin and mineral tablet should fulfil any need.

How to make the most of vitamins

Cooking in the microwave minimizes vitamin and mineral losses because they are cooked quickly in small amounts of water. Leave the skins on when you can and eat vegetables and fruit raw whenever possible. Vitamin losses continue after cooking, particularly when warm foods are left waiting around, so eat as soon as possible. Water-soluble vitamin C and B-group vitamins are easily lost or destroyed during storage, preparation and cooking. Choose fruit and vegetables in peak condition, store them in a cool dry place and eat as soon as possible. Tough, old vegetables have a lower vitamin content than fresh, and even the microwave won't revive their texture.

Vitamins and microwave cooking

Rapid microwave cooking times mean that fewer vitamins are destroyed. Most foods cook in their own juices or need only small amounts of water to keep them moist which means there is less likelihood that vitamins and minerals will leach out and be lost in the cooking water. Foods like fruit and vegetables can be cooked just before you need them and eaten immediately, before the vitamin content dwindles. A short burst in the microwave will yield more vitamin C-rich juice from citrus fruits. Precooked meals and leftovers can be chilled or frozen and reheated in the microwave with little loss of vitamins. The microwave is also ideal for blanching fruit and vegetables for the freezer.

GUIDE TO VITAMINS

Folic acid

Needed to produce healthy red blood cells. Deficiency causes a form of anaemia.
Good food sources liver, green leafy vegetables, pulses, wholemeal bread, cereals and oranges.

Pantothenic acid

Plays an important role in releasing energy from fat and carbohydrate.
Good food sources found in a wide variety of foods. Offal, eggs, cheese and nuts are particularly rich sources.

Thiamin (Vitamin B1)

Helps to release energy from carbohydrates.
Good food sources milk, offal, eggs, fruit, vegetables, wholegrain and fortified cereals including bread and breakfast cereals, pulses, nuts.

Riboflavin (Vitamin B2)

Needed for releasing energy from foods.
Good food sources milk, offal, eggs, cheese and yeast extract.

Niacin

Helps with the conversion of food to release energy.
Good food sources meat, fish, fortified breakfast cereals, vegetables and yeast extract.

Pyridoxin (Vitamin B6)

Helps the body utilise protein and is important for the formation of healthy red blood cells.
Good food sources liver, cereals, pulses, poultry.

Cobalamin (Vitamin B12)

Essential for the formation of healthy red blood cells. Deficiency causes a form of anaemia. Vegans may be at risk of deficiency and should eat fortified foods or take supplements.
Good food sources liver, meat, egg, fish, milk and cheese. Some foods are fortified with this vitamin.

Biotin

Essential for the metabolism of fat.
Good food sources offal, eggs, vegetables, cereals, fruit and nuts. It is also made by naturally occurring bacteria in the intestine.

Vitamin C (Ascorbic acid)

Needed for healthy connective tissue. Claims that large doses prevent or cure colds are unproven. Smokers, oral contraceptive users and people recovering from surgery have higher requirements.
Good food sources fresh fruit, particularly citrus fruits and blackcurrants, and vegetables, including potatoes.

Vitamin A (Retinol)

Needed for growth, good vision in dim light, healthy skin and surface tissues. Retinol is the active form of vitamin A but other substances in food including carotene can be converted into vitamin A by the body.
Good food sources dairy foods, liver, green leafy vegetables, yellow and orange fruits and vegetables such as carrots, tomatoes and peaches, butter and margarine.

Vitamin D (Cholecalciferol)

Needed for growth and the formation of healthy teeth and bones. Most of the body's supply comes from the action of sunlight on a substance in the skin.
Good food sources oily fish, eggs, butter. Margarine, some milk powders and yogurts are fortified with Vitamin D.

Vitamin E

Thought to be essential for muscular health and blood circulation.
Good food sources wheat germ, vegetable oils, some root vegetables, green leafy vegetables, cereals and nuts.

Vitamin K

Needed for the normal clotting of blood.
Good food sources cereals, pulses and green leafy vegetables. Some is also manufactured by bacteria in the intestine.

HEALTHY FOOD, FAST

Convenience foods are marvellous when time is short or you can't be bothered to prepare a meal from scratch. While there is no harm in eating them occasionally, many are overprocessed and contain unhealthy amounts of hidden fat, sugar or salt. With a microwave cooker, the problem of providing healthy fast food is solved. Healthy snacks and meals using mostly fresh foods—jacket potatoes, soups, fish and hot sandwiches for instance—are ready in no time at all. And that makes it less tempting to resort to convenience foods and takeaways.

One of the main advantages of a microwave cooker is that frozen foods, including ready-made dishes, can be thawed and cooked or reheated when they are wanted. There is less washing up too since meals can be cooked in and served from the same dish or even served on to plates and chilled for reheating later (ideal for busy families as the microwave is safe for older children to use provided they understand how to use the controls and use oven gloves for hot dishes).

Baby foods are quick and economical to prepare from fresh, wholesome ingredients—stir well to distribute the heat and check the temperature before feeding—and special diets or faddy eaters can be catered for without too much effort.

Look at labels

If you find it difficult to decide whether one food is a healthier choice than another, the label might give you a clue. Most prepacked foods must include certain information such as the name and description of the food, how to prepare it, the name and address of the manufacturer and in some cases a best before or sell-by date. Labels must also list the ingredients in the food in descending order of weight, including any additives. Get into the habit of reading food labels so you can avoid food with excessive amounts of sugar, salt or undesirable additives. More manufacturers are including helpful nutritional labelling on food packs. At the time of writing this book, the government was committed to the introduction of fat content labelling which should mean that in the future almost all foods will be labelled with the amount and type of fat they contain. Other nutritional information will still be given on a purely voluntary basis but will at least be presented in a uniform way.

AVOIDING ADDITIVES

Food additives—either natural or artificial—are used for a variety of different purposes. Some preserve, flavour or colour food while others like emulsifiers and stabilisers make certain manufacturing processes possible. Although the majority of additives are thought to be perfectly safe, some do cause unpleasant reactions in a small number of people. Healthy eating habits, including plenty of fresh and unprocessed foods, will automatically keep the level of additives you eat to a minimum but it is sensible to avoid additives whenever possible. Always read ingredient lists and choose foods free from artificial additives.

SLIMMING DOWN

Don't feel you have to lose weight to conform to fashionable ideals but remember for health reasons it is sensible to avoid being too fat. Being overweight increases the risk of disorders like heart disease, high blood pressure, adult onset diabetes, gallstones and hernias. If you need to lose weight, be realistic about your body and why you want to slim down—forget your fantasies and see losing weight as a way of staying healthy.

If you are overweight, you are eating (or have at some time eaten) more calories than your body needs. Different people need different numbers of calories but providing the number eaten is roughly the same as the body uses up, then your weight should stay about the same. The key to losing weight is to eat fewer calories than your body needs so it starts using up the stores of fat. It is tempting to go on crash diets that drastically cut food intake or restrict you to eating just a few foods but they don't work in the long-term. If you have tried them already, the chances are they didn't help you lose weight permanently and that is because they rarely tackle basic eating habits. Even if you lose weight rapidly in the first week or so it is due mostly to loss of body water rather than fat. So, face the fact that there are no miracle cures—the important point is to change the eating habits that probably caused the problem in the first place.

Fortunately, the best way to shift unwanted pounds and stay healthy is to adopt basically healthy eating habits. There are no forbidden foods but to lose weight it is particularly important to cut right down on sugary and fatty foods which are loaded with unnecessary calories. Eat plenty of fresh fruit and vegetables; choose lean meat (especially poultry, offal and game), white fish and seafood, low-fat cheeses and skimmed or semi-skimmed milk. Don't shun starchy fibre-rich foods like wholemeal bread, cereals, pasta and potatoes which are not that high in calories, contain a good range of nutrients and, most important, help you feel full and thoroughly satisfied.

All of the recipes in this book are suitable for slimmers and include a guide to how many calories they contain. Providing you don't exceed an average of about 1200 calories a day (1500 if you're a man), you should lose weight steadily. The important thing to remember is the overall balance of how many calories you eat over a week. If you eat too much one day just go more carefully the next.

After the first week, aim to lose about 0.5–1 kg (1–2 lb) a week. Once you have slimmed down, you will be able to increase your calorie intake without putting weight on again. But keep an eye on the scales—if you increase your calorie intake by too much your weight will start creeping up again. Get in the habit of taking some regular exercise, too, as it uses up calories, revs up the body's metabolism and helps you stay fit and healthy.

HEALTHY AND SLIM FOR LIFE

Good eating habits play a vital role in keeping a body healthy but remember that other factors like not smoking, only drinking alcohol in moderation and taking regular exercise are important too.

Your microwave won't automatically change unhealthy eating habits—that's up to you—but it can make a valuable contribution to a healthy diet by helping to get the best out of food.

If you have decided to adopt healthier eating habits, make changes gradually and choose ones that suit you—that way it is easier to keep to them until they are established habits. The more changes you make, the better, but a few changes are better than none at all.

SPECIAL INGREDIENTS

In the recipes, specific ingredients which are suitable for a healthy diet are suggested. You may not be familiar with some of these, so the more unusual ones are described below. Availability of these ingredients varies locally so where possible an alternative is given.

FATS AND OILS

Fats and oils are made up of fatty acids which are either saturated or unsaturated. Some fats are essential for health but too much saturated fat may increase the risk of heart disease, so it is preferable to use polyunsaturated or monounsaturated fats and oils. When buying margarine, look for those high in polyunsaturated fat and low in saturated fat. Choose polyunsaturated oils such as corn, sunflower, safflower, grapeseed, soya, sesame and olive. Less fat is needed for cooking in a microwave cooker because it is a moist method of cooking.

DAIRY PRODUCTS

Quark
A low- or medium-fat soft cheese, originally from Germany. Made from skimmed or whole milk or buttermilk, it may also include cream. It has a grainy texture and slightly acidic flavour. It is sold in cartons and is now available with added flavourings such as garlic and paprika. Different brands vary in calorie content, from 25–50 calories per 25 g (1 oz).

Fromage frais
The term covers a multitude of cheeses but basically refers to unripened, white soft cheeses.

Their fat content varies enormously from as little as 2% in some skimmed milk soft cheeses to at least 20% in full-fat soft cheeses and 45% or more in cream cheeses. Read the packet carefully to see exactly what you are getting. The varieties are interchangeable in most recipes and have a light, fresh clean taste.

Curd cheese
This has a smooth, creamy texture and is denser than most other varieties of soft cheese. Made from semi-skimmed milk, it is produced by a natural souring process without the addition of

rennet. It has a medium fat content and contains 54 calories per 25 g (1 oz). Curd cheese can be successfully substituted for cream cheese in many recipes in this book.

Ricotta

An Italian soft cheese made from the whey left over when producing other cheeses. It has a delicate, smooth flavour and is available from delicatessens. It contains 55 calories per 25 g (1 oz).

Mozzarella

This Italian cheese is traditionally made from buffalo milk but is now more often made from cows' milk. When fresh, it is very soft, dripping with buttermilk. It has a medium fat content and contains 87 calories per 25 g (1 oz).

Feta cheese

This is a moist, crumbly cheese originating from Greece. It is made from cows' or ewes' milk and has a medium fat content. It contains 54 calories per 25 g (1 oz). It has a distinctive taste and is very salty.

Yogurt

Yogurt, like milk, is an excellent source of calcium, protein and B vitamins and, because it contains lactic acid, is digested very quickly. It is very useful for thickening sauces and for making dressings and is a healthy alternative to cream and mayonnaise. There are many different types of yogurt available.

Whole milk yogurt   Contains about 4% fat and provides about 100 calories per 100 g (4 oz).

Low-fat yogurt   Made from skimmed milk with concentrated skimmed milk added to improve the consistency. It has a fat content of 0.5–2% and contains about 50 calories per 100 g (4 oz). Very low fat yogurt contains up to 0.5% fat.

Greek strained yogurt   Thick and creamy because it has a fat content of about 10%. It contains about 145 calories per 100 g (4 oz) and, although this is higher in calories than any other type of natural yogurt, it is still not as high as cream which contains 240–500 calories per 100 g (4 oz).

Buttermilk

Buttermilk is the liquid left over from butter making, so it contains very little fat. It has a thin consistency and makes a refreshing drink. It is a useful ingredient in sauces and soups. Contains 232 calories per 575 ml (1 pint) carton.

Smetana

This can be used as a substitute for cream and soured cream as it looks and tastes similar but has a lower fat content. There are two types of smetana available: standard smetana is about 6% fat and is made from skimmed milk, added milk solids and lactic culture, and richer creamed smetana which has a higher fat content of about 12%. Both types are sold in cartons in large supermarkets and delicatessens.

SOYA PRODUCTS

Tofu

Tofu, also known as bean curd, is made from a soya bean and water mixture which is strained and pressed to form white blocks. It is high in protein and very low in fat, making it a nutritious substitute for meat, fish and dairy produce. Used extensively in Chinese cooking, tofu is bland in flavour so always marinate before cooking or use in a well-flavoured dish. Look for it in cartons in the refrigerated sections of large supermarkets, in health and wholefood shops and in Chinese stores. There are several types available.

Silken tofu   Very soft and useful for making dressings and sauces.

Firm tofu   Made from pressed silken tofu which, as its name suggests, is much firmer than the silken variety. A naturally smoked and herb variety are also available. Cut into cubes and use in stir-fry type dishes.

Soft tofu   This has a texture between silken and firm tofu and can be used like firm tofu.

Soya milk

Soya milk is made from soya beans. It is easier to digest than cows' milk and is a useful substitute for people who are allergic to cows' milk. It contains about 370 calories per 568 ml (1 pint).

Sava (Vegan cheese)

This is an imitation hard cheese made from soya flour and a hard vegetable margarine. It is flavoured principally with yeast extract. Herb and/or garlic flavoured varieties are also available from some health food shops. Sava is best uncooked. It can be cooked but does not melt well.

FLAVOURINGS AND THICKENERS

Shoyu

This is pure soya sauce made from naturally fermented soya beans, salt and barley or wheat. Choose in preference to soya sauce which often contains additives.

Miso

A thick paste made from soya beans. It has a similar flavour to soya sauce. Use sparingly as it is very salty.

Tahini

A paste of ground sesame seeds. Use as a flavouring for sauces and dressings.

Carob

Carob powder is produced from the carob bean (also known as the locust bean) which come from a tree grown in the Mediterranean. Carob is used as a substitute for chocolate because it has a natural sweetness and contains no caffeine, less fat, more vitamins and more minerals than chocolate. It is also said to be less likely to cause migraine or teenage acne. It is available in sweetened and unsweetened bars. In cooking, use powdered carob as a substitute for cocoa powder and unsweetened carob bars as a substitute for chocolate.

Agar-agar

This is used as a setting agent and is the vegetarian substitute for animal gelatine. It is a tasteless white powder derived from seaweed and is available from health food shops.

GRAINS

All grains contain protein and, when mixed with other second class protein ingredients such as nuts or pulses, will provide good quality protein for healthy growth and repair of body tissue. The B vitamins and minerals such as calcium, iron and copper are to be found in all grains; some also contain vitamin E. One important constituent of grains and grain products is dietary fibre. This is found in useful amounts when the grains are left unrefined, that is, when their outer coating, or bran, is left intact.

KIPPER KEDGEREE (PAGE 22)

Wholewheat grains

The wholewheat grain is made up of the bran, the endosperm or starchy part, and the germ, which is the most nutritious but makes up only 2% of the grain. Contained in the germ are the vitamins and minerals. Wholewheat grains can be cooked to make an accompaniment to a main meal or a pudding.

Wheat germ

Wheat germ is the tiny nutritious part that has been separated from the main grain. It is consequently a highly concentrated source of B vitamins, vitamin E and minerals. If untreated, store in the refrigerator to prevent rancidity. Treated or stabilised wheat germ has been processed to prevent this. Wheat germ can be sprinkled over sweet dishes and cereals, and used in crumble toppings, coatings and cakes.

Burghul wheat

Also called bulgar or bulghur wheat, this is made from wholewheat grains that have been soaked and then baked until they crack into small yellow particles.

Pot barley

This is the barley grain with only the rough outer husk removed. It is also called Scotch or hulled barley. Pot barley can be bought in some health food shops. It is a healthier alternative to pearl barley which has both outer layers removed and so does not have the fibre content of pot barley. Cook in the same way as brown rice.

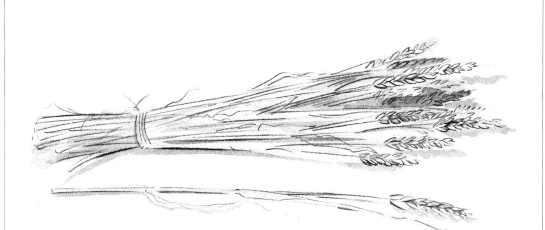

PASTINA AND SUMMER VEGETABLE SOUP (PAGE 28)

CHAPTER 1

Breakfasts

Herrings in Oatmeal

Serves 2
556 calories per serving

2 small herrings, filleted

salt and pepper

60 ml (4 level tbsp) medium oatmeal

30 ml (2 tbsp) polyunsaturated oil

5 ml (1 tsp) lemon juice

lemon wedges, to garnish

Herrings are a neglected fish, yet they are a good source of protein, the minerals calcium and phosphorus and, because they are oily fish, vitamins A and D.

1 Heat a large browning dish on HIGH for 5–8 minutes according to manufacturer's instructions.

2 Meanwhile, season the fish with salt and pepper to taste, then coat in the oatmeal.

3 Pour the oil into the browning dish, then quickly add the herrings. Microwave on HIGH for 1 minute, then turn them over and microwave on HIGH for 1–2 minutes, or until tender.

4 Sprinkle over the lemon juice. Serve immediately garnished with lemon wedges.

Griddle Scones

Makes 8
105 calories each

225 g (8 oz) self-raising wholemeal flour

pinch of salt

15 g ($\frac{1}{2}$ oz) polyunsaturated margarine

15 g ($\frac{1}{2}$ oz) light muscovado sugar

about 150 ml ($\frac{1}{4}$ pint) buttermilk

Although associated with teatime, these scones are perfect for breakfast. They are high in fibre, provided by the wholemeal flour.

1 Put the flour and salt into a bowl. Rub in the margarine then stir in the sugar. Add enough buttermilk to give a soft but manageable dough.

2 Knead lightly on a floured work surface, divide in two and roll into two rounds, 0.5 cm ($\frac{1}{4}$ inch) thick. Cut each round into four.

3 Heat a griddle, skillet or large browning dish on HIGH for about 5 minutes. Do not allow the dish to become too hot or the scones will burn. If necessary, allow the dish to cool slightly.

4 Quickly place four quarters on to the griddle and microwave on HIGH for $1\frac{1}{2}$ minutes. Turn the scones over and microwave on HIGH for a further 2 minutes. Repeat with the remaining scones, without reheating the browning dish. Eat while still hot, spread lightly with polyunsaturated margarine.

Dried Fruit Compote

Serves 4–6
158–105 calories per serving

125 g (4 oz) dried prunes

125 g (4 oz) dried apple rings

25 g (1 oz) seedless raisins

300 ml ($\frac{1}{2}$ pint) unsweetened apple juice

1 lemon

In this dish, there is no need to soak the fruit first, although you should leave the compote to stand for about 30 minutes before serving. Full of concentrated goodness, dried fruits are a good source of dietary fibre.

1 Put all the fruits into a large bowl. Pour over the apple juice with 300 ml ($\frac{1}{2}$ pint) water.

2 Using a potato peeler, thinly pare the lemon rind. Squeeze and strain the juice. Stir the rind into the fruit mixture with 30 ml (2 tbsp) lemon juice. Make sure all the fruit is under liquid, adding more water if necessary.

3 Cover, leaving a gap to let steam escape, and microwave on HIGH for 10 minutes until the fruits are almost tender, stirring occasionally.

4 Leave to stand for about 30 minutes before serving warm. Alternatively, leave to cool completely then chill well before serving.

Thick Fruit Porridge

Serves 4
298 calories per serving

568 ml (1 pint) skimmed milk

100 g (4 oz) porridge oats

25 g (1 oz) wheat germ

2 eating apples

50 g (2 oz) sultanas

This cereal dish is ideal to serve on a cold winter's day to sustain you through the morning. A high fibre breakfast, with the wheat germ in particular providing vitamin B.

1 Stir together the milk, oats and wheat germ in a medium bowl. Microwave on HIGH for 6 minutes or until boiling, stirring every minute.

2 Meanwhile, roughly chop but do not peel the apples, discarding the core.

3 Stir the apple and sultanas into the porridge and microwave on HIGH for 2 minutes, stirring frequently until thick. Serve hot, with honey to taste.

Frumenty

Serves 4
300 calories per serving

225 g (8 oz) wholewheat grain, soaked overnight

50 g (2 oz) no-soak dried apricots

50 g (2 oz) dates

568 ml (1 pint) skimmed milk

50 g (2 oz) sultanas

2.5 ml ($\frac{1}{2}$ level tsp) ground cinnamon

2.5 ml ($\frac{1}{2}$ level tsp) freshly grated nutmeg

This old English breakfast dish is based on wholewheat grain which contains useful amounts of fibre, vitamins B and E and minerals, such as calcium, potassium and iron.

1 Drain the wholewheat and put in a large bowl. Roughly chop the apricots and dates and add to the bowl with all the remaining ingredients.

2 Microwave on HIGH for about 25 minutes until the wheat is tender and most of the milk has been absorbed. Stir frequently during cooking.

3 Leave the frumenty to stand for 2–3 minutes, then serve hot with low-fat natural yogurt.

Fluffy Scrambled Eggs

Serves 2
95 calories per serving

4 eggs

60 ml (4 tbsp) skimmed milk

salt and pepper

It is generally agreed that it is important to reduce your intake of saturated fat rather than cut out cholesterol-rich foods specifically. Since eggs are particularly high in cholesterol, nutritionists recommend we eat no more than six a week.

1 Break the eggs into a medium bowl and whisk together. Whisk in the milk and salt and pepper to taste.

2 Microwave on HIGH for 1 minute or until the mixture begins to set around the edge of the bowl. Whisk vigorously to incorporate the set egg mixture.

3 Microwave on HIGH for a further 1–2 minutes, whisking vigorously every 30 seconds until the eggs are just set but still very soft. Whisk again and serve on hot wholemeal toast.

To serve 4

Double all the ingredients.
In step 2, microwave on HIGH for 2 minutes or until the mixture begins to set around the edge.
In step 3, microwave on HIGH for 2 minutes or until the eggs are just set.

Egg Ramekins

Serves 2
105 calories per serving

1 large tomato

salt and pepper

2 eggs

30 ml (2 tbsp) low-fat natural yogurt

large pinch of mustard powder

few drops of Worcestershire sauce

An interesting new way to serve eggs for breakfast. If you don't have ramekin dishes, use two sturdy ovenproof mugs or cups instead.

1 Roughly chop the tomato and divide between two 150 ml ($\frac{1}{4}$ pint) ramekin dishes. Season with salt and pepper to taste.

2 Carefully break one egg into each ramekin and prick each yolk twice, using a cocktail stick or a sharp knife. Microwave on MEDIUM for $1\frac{1}{2}$–2 minutes or until the egg white is just set.

3 Meanwhile, mix the yogurt, mustard and Worcestershire sauce together. Spoon on top of the eggs and microwave on HIGH for 30 seconds.

4 Grind a little black pepper on top of each ramekin. Leave to stand for 2 minutes, then serve with wholemeal toast.

Kipper Kedgeree

Serves 6
182 calories per serving

225 g (8 oz) naturally smoked kipper fillet

30 ml (2 tbsp) skimmed milk

15 ml (1 tbsp) polyunsaturated oil

1 medium onion, skinned and chopped

5 ml (1 level tsp) mild curry powder

225 g (8 oz) long-grain brown rice, cooked

1 egg, hard-boiled and chopped

175 g (6 oz) peeled prawns

30 ml (2 tbsp) chopped fresh parsley

10 ml (2 tsp) lemon juice

pepper

chopped fresh parsley

Make sure that you buy naturally smoked kippers rather than the kind that have been artificially coloured. For convenience, cook the rice the day before.

1 Put the kipper fillet and milk in a large shallow dish. Cover, leaving a gap to let steam escape, and microwave on HIGH for 3–4 minutes or until the fish flakes easily when tested with a fork. Set aside.

2 Put the oil and onion in an ovenproof serving dish and microwave on HIGH for 5 minutes or until softened. Stir in the curry powder and microwave on HIGH for 1 minute.

3 Add the rice to the onion with the egg, prawns, parsley, lemon juice and pepper to taste.

4 Flake the kipper and stir carefully into the rice mixture with 30 ml (2 tbsp) of the poaching liquid.

5 Microwave on HIGH for 2–3 minutes until heated through, stirring once. Serve hot, garnished with chopped parsley.

Kipper with Tomato

Serves 1
385 calories per serving

1 kipper fillet, about 175 g (6 oz)

squeeze of lemon juice

pinch of ground mace

black pepper

1 large tomato

A really quick yet tasty breakfast, with minimal preparatory fuss as the kippers are cooked on their serving plate. Make sure the kipper has not been artificially coloured.

1 Place the kipper fillet towards the edge of an ovenproof dinner plate. Sprinkle with the lemon juice and season with mace and black pepper to taste.

2 Cut the tomato into quarters, cutting almost through to the base but keeping the tomato whole. Place on the plate with the kipper.

3 Cover loosely with absorbent kitchen paper and microwave on HIGH for 2–3 minutes or until the kipper is hot. Serve immediately with wholemeal bread.

Creamy Kidneys with Mushrooms

Serves 4
192 calories per serving

6 lamb's kidneys

100 g (4 oz) flat mushrooms

15 ml (1 tbsp) polyunsaturated oil

30 ml (2 tbsp) Greek strained yogurt

5 ml (1 level tsp) wholegrain mustard

15 ml (1 tbsp) chopped fresh herbs, such as marjoram, parsley or chervil

salt and pepper

4 slices of wholemeal toast

This variation, on a traditional theme, provides a quick, healthy and satisfying start to the day. Serve this kidney dish as a special treat at the weekend.

1 Skin the kidneys if necessary. Cut each one in half lengthways and snip out the cores with scissors. Slice the kidneys finely and set aside.

2 Remove the stalks from the mushrooms and peel the caps if necessary. Slice them finely.

3 Heat a large browning dish on HIGH for 5–8 minutes or according to manufacturer's instructions.

4 Add the oil, kidneys and mushrooms to the dish and stir well. Microwave on HIGH for 3 minutes or until the kidneys are just tender, stirring once or twice.

5 Stir in the yogurt, mustard and herbs and season with salt and pepper to taste. Microwave on HIGH for a further 2 minutes or until heated through.

6 To serve, place a slice of toast on individual serving plates and pile the kidney mixture on top. Serve at once.

Bran Muffins

Makes 8
90 calories per muffin

50 g (2 oz) bran

75 g (3 oz) plain wholemeal flour

7.5 ml (1½ level tsp) baking powder

1 egg, beaten

300 ml (½ pint) skimmed milk

30 ml (2 tbsp) clear honey

These fibre-rich muffins are best served warm straight from the oven. Serve them on their own or to accompany another breakfast dish.

1 Put the bran, flour and baking powder in a bowl and mix together. Add the egg, milk and honey and stir until well mixed.

2 Divide the mixture between an eight-hole bun tray. Microwave on HIGH for 5–6 minutes until firm to the touch.

3 Leave to stand for 5 minutes. Split each muffin in half horizontally and serve spread lightly with polyunsaturated margarine.

Hot Breakfast Nog

Serves 1
150 calories per serving

5 ml (1 level tsp) carob powder

300 ml (½ pint) skimmed milk

5 ml (1 level tsp) fine oatmeal

5 ml (1 tsp) clear honey

5 ml (1 level tsp) wheat germ

This drink makes a warming and nourishing start to the day. It is flavoured and partly sweetened by the naturally sweet carob powder, a healthy substitute for cocoa and chocolate. Have a piece of fresh fruit to follow to provide a more filling breakfast.

1 Put the carob powder, milk, oatmeal and honey in a large mug. Microwave on HIGH for 1½–2 minutes or until hot.

2 Sprinkle over the wheat germ and drink while still hot.

NOTE: To serve more than one person, simply increase the quantities accordingly and proceed as in step 1.
Microwave 2 cups for 3–3½ minutes and 4 cups for 5–8½ minutes.

Soups

Spinach Soup

Serves 4
75 calories per serving

15 ml (1 tbsp) polyunsaturated oil

1 large onion, skinned and chopped

450 g (1 lb) fresh spinach, trimmed and roughly chopped or 225 g (8 oz) frozen spinach

15 ml (1 level tbsp) wholemeal flour

600 ml (1 pint) boiling chicken or vegetable stock

freshly grated nutmeg

salt and pepper

60 ml (4 tbsp) low-fat natural yogurt

When buying fresh spinach choose bright, green leaves and avoid any that are yellow or wilted. Always wash the leaves thoroughly in several changes of water because spinach collects dirt which will give an unpleasant gritty texture to the soup.

1 Put the oil and onion in a medium bowl. Cover, leaving a gap to let steam escape, and microwave on HIGH for 5–7 minutes until softened.

2 Add the spinach, re-cover and microwave on HIGH for 3–4 minutes, or 8–9 minutes until thawed if using frozen spinach, stirring occasionally.

3 Sprinkle in the flour and microwave on HIGH for 30 seconds, then gradually stir in the stock. Season with nutmeg and salt and pepper to taste. Microwave on HIGH for about 4 minutes until boiling, stirring occasionally.

4 Leave to cool slightly, then purée the soup in a blender or food processor. Pour the soup back into the bowl and microwave on HIGH for 2 minutes until boiling. Ladle the soup into warmed bowls and swirl a spoonful of yogurt into each before serving.

Tomato and Plum Soup

Serves 4
74 calories per serving

1 small onion, skinned and finely chopped

450 g (1 lb) red tomatoes, roughly chopped

350 g (12 oz) red plums, stoned and roughly chopped

300 ml ($\frac{1}{2}$ pint) fresh tomato juice

300 ml ($\frac{1}{2}$ pint) boiling chicken stock

10 ml (2 tsp) chopped fresh basil or pinch of dried

salt and pepper

60 ml (4 tbsp) buttermilk

If, for convenience and to save time, you use a stock cube to make the chicken stock, use about a quarter less of the cube than recommended and do not add extra salt to the soup as stock cubes tend to be salty.

1 Put the onion, tomatoes and plums in a large bowl. Cover, leaving a gap to let steam escape, and microwave on HIGH for 10–15 minutes or until very soft, stirring occasionally.

2 Add the tomato juice, stock and basil. Transfer to a blender or food processor and work until smooth. Pass through a sieve to remove any seeds. Return to the bowl and season with salt and pepper to taste.

3 Microwave on HIGH for 1–2 minutes or until heated through. Serve hot or chilled, with the buttermilk spooned over and garnished with basil sprigs.

Walnut Soup

Serves 4–6
243–162 calories per serving

175 g (6 oz) walnuts

1 garlic clove, skinned

600 ml (1 pint) boiling
vegetable stock

150 ml ($\frac{1}{4}$ pint) low-fat natural
yogurt

salt and pepper

chopped walnuts, to garnish

This unusual, subtle-tasting soup, made simply using walnuts, stock, yogurt and garlic, can be served hot or cold. Walnuts are high in potassium, calcium, magnesium, iron and zinc.

1 Put the walnuts and garlic in a blender or food processor and work until finely crushed. If using a blender, you may need to add a little of the stock to blend the walnuts. Very gradually pour in the stock until smooth.

2 Pour the soup into a large bowl. Microwave on HIGH for 5 minutes until boiling, stirring occasionally.

3 Stir in the yogurt and season with salt and pepper to taste. Serve hot or cold, garnished with chopped walnuts.

Cauliflower Soup

Serves 4–6
90–60 calories per serving

15 ml (1 tbsp) polyunsaturated
oil

1 small onion, skinned and
finely chopped

1 small garlic clove, skinned
and finely chopped

1 small cauliflower, trimmed

450 ml ($\frac{3}{4}$ pint) boiling
vegetable stock

450 ml ($\frac{3}{4}$ pint) skimmed milk

freshly grated nutmeg

salt and pepper

snipped fresh chives, to garnish

A low-calorie soup to keep slimmers on the straight and narrow. It makes a good light summer starter too.

1 Put the oil, onion and garlic in a large bowl. Cover, leaving a gap to let steam escape, and microwave on HIGH for 4–5 minutes until softened, stirring occasionally.

2 Meanwhile, divide the cauliflower into small florets, discarding the stalks. Add the florets to the bowl with the stock, milk, nutmeg and salt and pepper to taste. Microwave on HIGH for 15–20 minutes until the cauliflower is very tender, stirring occasionally.

3 Leave to cool slightly, then purée the soup in a blender or food processor.

4 Pour the soup back into the bowl and microwave on HIGH for 2 minutes or until hot. Ladle the soup into warmed bowls, sprinkle with snipped chives and serve with wholemeal bread, if liked.

Green Split Pea Soup

Serves 4–6
183–122 calories per serving

2 leeks, finely chopped and washed

2 celery sticks, trimmed and finely chopped

2 carrots, scrubbed and finely chopped

1 garlic clove, skinned and crushed

15 ml (1 tbsp) olive oil

175 g (6 oz) dried green split peas

freshly grated nutmeg

salt and pepper

chopped fresh parsley, to garnish

Green split peas are high in fibre, B vitamins and protein but lack certain amino acids. However, serving this soup with wholemeal rolls provides the extra amino acids and produces a well-balanced meal to serve on winter days.

1 Put the leeks, celery, carrots, garlic and oil in a large bowl. Microwave on HIGH for 5 minutes.

2 Stir in the split peas and 900 ml (1½ pints) boiling water and mix well together. Cover, leaving a gap to let steam escape, and microwave on HIGH for 25 minutes until the peas are very soft, stirring occasionally.

3 When the split peas are cooked, turn the mixture into a blender or food processor and work until smooth. Season with nutmeg and salt and pepper to taste and pour into an ovenproof serving bowl.

4 Return the soup to the cooker and microwave on HIGH for 3 minutes or until the soup is hot. Garnish with chopped parsley and serve the soup immediately with warm wholemeal rolls.

Pastina and Summer Vegetable Soup

Serves 4
127 calories per serving

15 ml (1 tbsp) olive oil

100 g (4 oz) new carrots, scrubbed and sliced

100 g (4 oz) French beans, trimmed and cut in half

225 g (8 oz) young peas, shelled

50 g (2 oz) pastina

900 ml (1½ pints) boiling vegetable stock

30 ml (2 tbsp) chopped fresh mint

4 lettuce leaves, finely shredded

salt and pepper

Pastina is the general name used for the tiny pasta shapes that are usually cooked in soups. If you cannot obtain them, use a larger size but remember, the cooking time will be longer.

1 Put the oil, carrots, beans and peas in a large bowl. Cover, leaving a gap to let steam escape, and microwave on HIGH for 2 minutes, stirring once.

2 Add the pastina and stock. Re-cover and microwave on HIGH for 10 minutes or until the pasta and vegetables are tender.

3 Stir in the mint and lettuce and season with salt and pepper to taste. Microwave on HIGH for 1 minute or until the lettuce is just wilted. Serve hot.

Barley and Chick Pea Soup

Serves 4
197 calories per serving

15 ml (1 tbsp) olive oil

1 large onion, skinned and chopped

1 garlic clove, skinned and chopped

50 g (2 oz) pot barley

900 ml (1½ pints) boiling vegetable stock

2.5 ml (½ level tsp) ground turmeric

2.5 ml (½ level tsp) concentrated mint sauce

100 g (4 oz) fresh spinach, washed, trimmed and shredded

397 g (14 oz) can chick peas, drained and rinsed

salt and pepper

60 ml (4 tbsp) set natural yogurt (optional)

10 ml (2 level tsp) sesame seeds, toasted (optional)

Chick peas add fibre and protein to this tasty soup. Canned chick peas are used for convenience but dried chick peas could be cooked separately and used instead.

1 Put the oil, onion and garlic in a large bowl. Microwave on HIGH for 2 minutes, stirring once.

2 Add the barley, stock, turmeric and concentrated mint sauce. Cover, leaving a gap to let steam escape, and microwave on HIGH for 20 minutes until the barley is tender, stirring occasionally.

3 Stir in the spinach and chick peas and season with salt and pepper to taste. Re-cover and microwave on HIGH for 2–3 minutes or until heated through.

4 Pour into four soup bowls. Top each bowl with a spoonful of yogurt and sprinkle with sesame seeds if liked. Serve immediately.

Hearty White Fish Soup

Serves 4–6
247–164 calories per serving

2 large onions, skinned and finely sliced

225 g (8 oz) new potatoes, scrubbed and thinly sliced

2 garlic cloves, skinned and crushed

15 ml (1 tbsp) olive oil

1 fresh green chilli, seeded and chopped

1 red pepper, seeded and chopped

150 ml ($\frac{1}{4}$ pint) dry white wine

750 ml ($1\frac{1}{4}$ pints) boiling fish or vegetable stock

700 g ($1\frac{1}{2}$ lb) firm white fish such as cod or haddock, skinned

salt and pepper

45 ml (3 tbsp) chopped fresh mixed herbs

This fish soup is substantial enough to be served as a main course for a light lunch or supper. Accompany with chunks of fresh granary bread to mop up the juices.

1 Put the onions, potatoes, garlic, oil and chilli in a large bowl. Microwave on HIGH for 2 minutes.

2 Stir in the red pepper, wine and stock. Cover, leaving a gap to let steam escape, and microwave on HIGH for 10–12 minutes or until the potato is tender.

3 Meanwhile, cut the fish into large chunks and stir into the soup. Re-cover and microwave on HIGH for 3 minutes or until the fish is cooked. Season with salt and pepper to taste and stir in the herbs. Serve immediately.

Chinese-style Chicken and Beansprout Soup

Serves 4
87 calories per serving

1 red pepper, seeded and very thinly shredded

100 g (4 oz) button mushrooms, thinly sliced

45 ml (3 tbsp) shoyu sauce

45 ml (3 tbsp) dry sherry

1.25 cm ($\frac{1}{2}$ inch) piece fresh root ginger, peeled and grated

5 ml (1 tsp) clear honey

100 g (4 oz) cooked chicken breast, skinned

4 spring onions, trimmed

50 g (2 oz) beansprouts

pepper

Serve this quick and easy soup as a light meal on its own or as part of a Chinese-style meal. Shoyu sauce is naturally fermented soya sauce made from soya beans and is preferable to the commercial soya sauce which often contains sugar and additives.

1 Put the pepper into a large bowl with the mushrooms, shoyu sauce, sherry, ginger, honey and 750 ml ($1\frac{1}{4}$ pints) boiling water. Microwave on HIGH for 4–5 minutes until the pepper is softened.

2 Meanwhile, thinly shred the chicken and spring onions. Add to the soup with the beansprouts, season with pepper to taste and microwave on HIGH for 5 minutes until heated through, stirring occasionally. Serve hot.

Vegetable and Oatmeal Broth

Serves 4–6

83–55 calories per serving

100 g (4 oz) sweetcorn kernels

1 medium onion, skinned and finely chopped

175 g (6 oz) swede, peeled and finely diced

2 medium carrots, scrubbed and finely diced

1 medium leek, trimmed and sliced

900 ml (1½ pints) boiling vegetable stock

25 g (1 oz) fine oatmeal

45 ml (3 tbsp) chopped fresh parsley

salt and pepper

If served with crusty wholemeal bread or rolls, this very low-calorie broth makes a hearty supper dish.

1 Put the corn, onion, swede, carrot, leek and 300 ml (½ pint) of the vegetable stock in a large bowl. Cover, leaving a gap to let steam escape, and microwave on HIGH for 12–15 minutes until the vegetables are tender.

2 Sprinkle in the oatmeal and stir together. Pour in the remaining vegetable stock and parsley and season with salt and pepper to taste.

3 Microwave on HIGH for 5 minutes or until boiling and thickened, stirring occasionally. Serve hot.

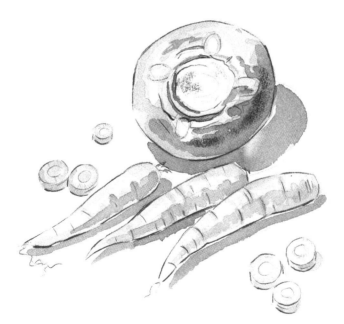

CHAPTER 3

Starters

BARLEY AND CHICK PEA SOUP (PAGE 29)

Red Lentil and Cheese Pâté

Serves 4–6
116–78 calories per serving

finely grated rind and juice of 1 orange

1 bay leaf

125 g (4 oz) red split lentils

125 g (4 oz) low-fat quark

1 garlic clove, skinned and crushed

15 ml (1 tbsp) chopped fresh mixed herbs, such as parsley, chives and dill

2.5 ml (½ level tsp) paprika

freshly grated nutmeg

salt and pepper

paprika, to garnish

Quark is a pure milk product originating from Germany. It is a low-fat, soft cheese with a smooth texture and slightly acidic flavour. It provides a low-fat, low–calorie alternative to full-fat soft cheese and is available from health food shops and most major supermarkets.

1 Put the orange rind and juice, bay leaf, lentils and 300 ml (½ pint) boiling water in a large bowl. Microwave on HIGH for 15–16 minutes or until the lentils are very soft and all the liquid is absorbed.

2 Remove the bay leaf, add the quark, garlic, herbs and paprika and beat together until smooth. Season with nutmeg and salt and pepper to taste.

3 Spoon the pâté into a serving dish, cover and refrigerate for at least 1 hour or until required. Serve sprinkled with a little paprika and accompany with slices of pumpernickel bread.

Chicken Liver and Green Peppercorn Pâté

Serves 4
133 calories per serving

15 ml (1 tbsp) polyunsaturated oil

1 medium onion, skinned and finely chopped

225 g (8 oz) chicken livers

1 small garlic clove, skinned and finely chopped

10 ml (2 level tsp) green peppercorns in brine, drained

60 ml (4 tbsp) Greek strained yogurt

salt

This delicious, smooth pâté could also be served as a cold, light lunch with a lightly dressed mixed green or tomato salad.

1 Put the oil and onion in a medium bowl. Cover, leaving a gap to let steam escape, and microwave on HIGH for 5–7 minutes until softened, stirring occasionally.

2 Meanwhile trim the chicken livers, cutting away any ducts and gristle, then cut into small pieces. Stir the livers and garlic into the onion. Re-cover and microwave on HIGH for about 3 minutes until the chicken livers are cooked, stirring occasionally.

3 Transfer to a blender or food processor. Add the green peppercorns, yogurt and salt to taste. Work until the chicken livers are smooth and the peppercorns lightly crushed.

4 Turn into a serving dish and chill for at least 2 hours. Serve with wholemeal toast.

AUBERGINE AND YOGURT PURÉE (PAGE 37)

Fresh Spinach and Mushroom Pâté

Serves 4–6
Makes 12 slices
50 calories per slice

450 g (1 lb) fresh spinach, washed and trimmed

15 ml (1 tbsp) olive oil

1 garlic clove, skinned and crushed

1 small onion, skinned and finely chopped

350 g (12 oz) mushrooms, finely chopped

finely grated rind and juice of 1 lemon

salt and pepper

freshly grated nutmeg

100 g (4 oz) wholemeal breadcrumbs

50 g (2 oz) low-fat soft cheese

Not only is the flavour and colour of fresh spinach retained when cooked in a microwave but the nutritional value is preserved because it is cooked for a very short time in just the water clinging to the leaves after washing. Do not try to make this pâté with frozen spinach, because it is too difficult to line the loaf dish with frozen spinach leaves.

1 Put the spinach with just the water that clings to the leaves in a large bowl. Microwave on HIGH for 4 minutes or until wilted.

2 Use half of the spinach to line a 700 g (1½ lb) microwave loaf dish. Chop the remaining spinach and set aside.

3 Put the oil, garlic, onion, mushrooms and lemon rind and juice in a large shallow dish. Cover, leaving a gap to let steam escape, and microwave on HIGH for 8–10 minutes or until the onions and mushrooms are very soft.

4 Season with salt, pepper and nutmeg to taste. Stir in the breadcrumbs, cheese and remaining spinach.

5 Spoon into the loaf dish and pack down well using the back of a spoon. Fold the spinach leaves over the mushroom mixture.

6 Leave to cool, then chill for at least 1 hour. To serve, turn out and cut into thick slices.

Corn-on-the-Cob with Herb Vinaigrette

Serves 4
185 calories per serving

4 corn-on-the-cob

15 ml (1 tbsp) polyunsaturated oil

15 ml (1 tbsp) lemon juice

30 ml (2 tbsp) chopped fresh mixed herbs

salt and pepper

Sweetcorn is a rich source of fibre and makes a very healthy starter when served with this low-fat dressing instead of the usual lashings of butter.

1 Peel back the husks from the corn and remove the silk, then pull back the husks again to cover. If the corn is without husks, wrap separately in greaseproof paper.

2 Place the corn cobs side by side in a shallow dish. Microwave on HIGH for 8–10 minutes until the corn is tender, turning and repositioning two or three times during cooking.

3 Meanwhile, whisk the oil, lemon juice and herbs together and season with salt and pepper to taste.

4 When the corn is cooked, place on four warmed serving plates and gently pull back the husks or remove the greaseproof paper. Pour a little dressing over each cob and serve immediately.

Mushrooms à la Grecque

Serves 6
46 calories per serving

1 medium onion, skinned and finely chopped

1 garlic clove, skinned and crushed

30 ml (2 level tbsp) tomato purée

150 ml ($\frac{1}{4}$ pint) dry red wine

15 ml (1 level tbsp) coriander seeds, finely crushed

2.5 ml ($\frac{1}{2}$ level tsp) light muscovado sugar

2.5 ml ($\frac{1}{2}$ level tsp) dried oregano

700 g (1$\frac{1}{2}$ lb) button mushrooms

225 g (8 oz) tomatoes, cut into small wedges

45 ml (3 tbsp) chopped fresh coriander

salt and pepper

For a really authentic Greek flavour, always use fresh coriander in this chilled 'Greek-style' starter. The wholemeal pitta bread may be warmed in the microwave for 20–30 seconds, just before serving. These mushrooms are also good served as a side dish.

1 Put the onion, garlic, tomato purée, wine, coriander seeds, sugar and oregano in a large bowl. Microwave on HIGH for 4 minutes or until boiling, then stir and microwave on HIGH for a further 2 minutes.

2 Add the mushrooms, tomatoes and 15 ml (1 tbsp) of the chopped coriander. Cover, leaving a gap to let steam escape, and microwave on HIGH for 10 minutes until the mushrooms are tender, stirring once. Season with salt and pepper to taste. Spoon into a serving dish and sprinkle with the remaining chopped coriander.

3 Leave to cool, then chill for at least 1 hour. Serve cold with warm wholemeal pitta bread.

Turkish Aubergines with Tomatoes

Serves 4–6
63–42 calories per serving

2 aubergines, total weight about 900 g (2 lb), with stalks on

5 ml (1 tsp) olive oil

1 large onion, skinned and thinly sliced

2 garlic cloves, skinned and crushed

4 large ripe tomatoes, chopped

1 green pepper, seeded and chopped

30 ml (2 level tbsp) tomato purée

5 ml (1 level tsp) ground allspice

5 ml (1 level tsp) ground cinnamon

1.25 ml ($\frac{1}{4}$ level tsp) cayenne pepper (optional)

45 ml (3 tbsp) chopped fresh parsley

salt and pepper

Similar to a Turkish recipe called Imam Bayildi which contains a lot of oil, this low-calorie dish is eaten cold with bread as an unusual first course.

1 Rub the aubergines with the olive oil and prick well all over with a fork. Place on a double thickness of absorbent kitchen paper. Microwave on HIGH for 8 minutes. Turn over and microwave on HIGH for a further 6–8 minutes or until the aubergines are very soft.

2 Put the onion, garlic, tomatoes, green pepper, tomato purée, allspice, cinnamon and cayenne pepper in a large bowl with 100 ml (4 fl oz) water. Cover, leaving a gap to let steam escape, and microwave on HIGH for 15–20 minutes or until the onion is soft, stirring once. Stir in half of the parsley and season with salt and pepper to taste.

3 Transfer the aubergines to a shallow serving dish and make about five slashes along the length of each. Fan them out, leaving the stalk intact. Spoon over the filling. Cover, leaving a gap to let steam escape, and microwave on HIGH for 5 minutes.

4 Leave to cool for 1 hour, then chill for at least 2 hours. Serve garnished with the remaining chopped parsley.

Ramekins of Smoked Trout

Serves 4
140 calories per serving

one 250 g (9 oz) smoked trout

150 g (5 oz) low-fat soft cheese

45 ml (3 tbsp) low-fat natural yogurt

15 ml (1 level tbsp) horseradish sauce

2 egg yolks

pepper

1 egg white

The mixture for this elegant fish starter should be microwaved until set around the edges but still soft in the centre.

1 Flake the fish, discarding skin and bones, and put in a bowl. Add the cheese, yogurt, horseradish, egg yolks and pepper to taste and beat together.

2 Whisk the egg white until stiff but not dry, then fold into the fish mixture.

3 Spoon the mixture into four 150 ml ($\frac{1}{4}$ pint) ramekin dishes. Microwave on HIGH for 4 minutes or until lightly set. Serve with wholemeal bread.

Stuffed Mushrooms

Serves 4–6
116 calories per serving

12 medium cup mushrooms

15 ml (1 tbsp) olive oil

1 garlic clove, skinned and crushed

finely grated rind and juice of 1 lemon

50 g (2 oz) fresh wholemeal breadcrumbs

25 g (1 oz) porridge oats

30 ml (2 tbsp) chopped fresh parsley

30 ml (2 tbsp) grated fresh Parmesan cheese

salt and pepper

fresh herb sprigs, to garnish

Medium-sized cup mushrooms are the most suitable for this recipe, but if you have difficulty in finding them use large, flat mushrooms instead.

1 Remove the mushroom stalks and finely chop them. Place the chopped stalks in a small bowl with the oil, garlic, lemon rind and half of the lemon juice. Cover, leaving a gap to let steam escape, and microwave on HIGH for 1–2 minutes until softened.

2 Stir in the breadcrumbs, oats, parsley and Parmesan cheese. Season with salt and pepper to taste.

3 Arrange the mushroom caps around the edge of a large shallow dish and spoon the stuffing on to each.

4 Pour the remaining lemon juice into the dish. Cover, leaving a gap to let steam escape, and microwave on HIGH for 5–6 minutes until the mushrooms are tender. Serve immediately, garnished with herbs.

Aubergine and Yogurt Purée

Serves 4
48 calories per serving

1 aubergine, total weight about 450 g (1 lb)

5 ml (1 tsp) polyunsaturated oil

1–2 garlic cloves, skinned and crushed

6 black olives, stoned and roughly chopped

juice of ½ lemon

150 ml (¼ pint) low-fat natural yogurt

Whole aubergines cook to perfection in the microwave and instead of turning brown, as in conventional cooking, they retain their delicate colour. Serve this interesting purée as a pâté or dip.

1 Rub the aubergine with the oil and prick well all over with a fork. Place on absorbent kitchen paper. Microwave on HIGH for 8 minutes or until tender, turning over once during cooking.

2 Leave to stand for 5 minutes then chop roughly, discarding the stalk. Put in a blender or food processor with the remaining ingredients and work until smooth.

3 Turn the purée into a bowl and leave to cool. Serve with wholemeal pitta bread, toast or crudités.

Spicy Prawns

Serves 6
88 calories per serving

1 small onion, skinned and finely chopped

1 garlic clove, skinned and chopped

3 large tomatoes, roughly chopped

2.5 cm (1 inch) piece fresh root ginger, peeled and crushed

2.5 ml (½ level tsp) ground coriander

2.5 ml (½ level tsp) ground cumin

15 ml (1 tbsp) red wine vinegar

5 ml (1 level tsp) tomato purée

450 g (1 lb) peeled prawns

salt and pepper

chopped fresh coriander, to garnish

These prawns taste delicious when served with grilled poppadums. The sauce can be prepared in advance, and the prawns added and heated through just before serving.

1 Put the onion, garlic, tomatoes, ginger, coriander, cumin, vinegar and tomato purée in a medium bowl. Microwave on HIGH for 10 minutes until thickened and reduced, stirring occasionally.

2 Add the prawns and stir together. Microwave on HIGH for 2–3 minutes until the prawns are heated through, stirring once. Season with salt and pepper to taste. Garnish with chopped coriander and serve hot with poppadums.

Smoked Haddock Mousses

Serves 6
83 calories per serving

350 g (12 oz) smoked haddock fillet

100 g (4 oz) cottage or curd cheese

150 ml (¼ pint) low-fat natural yogurt

grated rind and juice of ½ lemon

15 ml (1 tbsp) chopped fresh parsley

pepper

5 ml (1 level tsp) gelatine

lemon slices, to garnish

Smoked fish has a high salt content so only eat it occasionally and do not add extra salt to the recipe being used. These low-calorie mousses are served chilled.

1 Put the haddock in a shallow dish with 30 ml (2 tbsp) water. Cover, leaving a gap to let steam escape, and microwave on HIGH for 3 minutes or until the fish is tender.

2 Drain and flake the fish, discarding the skin and bones, and put in a blender or food processor. Add the cheese, yogurt, lemon rind, parsley and pepper to taste and work until smooth.

3 Put the lemon juice in a small bowl and sprinkle in the gelatine. Microwave on LOW for 1–1½ minutes or until the gelatine has dissolved, stirring occasionally. Add to the fish mixture and mix well together.

4 Divide the fish mixture equally between six individual ramekin dishes. Chill for at least 1 hour before serving.

5 Garnish with lemon slices and, if liked, turn the mousses out on to individual plates. Serve with toasted wholemeal bread.

Scallops with Tomato Sauce

Serves 4
135 calories per serving

15 ml (1 tbsp) polyunsaturated oil

½ small onion, skinned and finely chopped

1 garlic clove, skinned and crushed

227 g (8 oz) can tomatoes

15 ml (1 tbsp) dry white wine

30 ml (2 tbsp) chopped fresh basil

2.5 ml (½ level tsp) light muscovado sugar

salt and pepper

8 medium shelled scallops

basil sprigs, to garnish

This hot starter is easy to prepare, especially as the tomato sauce can be made in advance and then reheated before serving with the scallops.

1 To make the sauce, put the oil, onion and garlic in a medium bowl. Cover, leaving a gap to let steam escape, and microwave on HIGH for 3–4 minutes or until the onion has softened.

2 Stir in the tomatoes with their juice, wine, basil, sugar and salt and pepper to taste. Re-cover and microwave on HIGH for 10 minutes or until the sauce has thickened, stirring once or twice during the cooking time.

3 Leave to cool slightly, then purée the sauce in a blender or food processor.

4 Remove the tough muscle from each scallop which is found opposite the coral. Cut the corals from the scallops and set aside. Slice the white part across into two discs.

5 Arrange the white parts in a circle in a large shallow dish. Cover, leaving a gap to let steam escape, and microwave on HIGH for 2 minutes until the scallops are just opaque.

6 Add the reserved corals and microwave on HIGH for a further 1 minute until the corals are tender.

7 Drain the scallops and put in four scallop shells or on individual plates. Spoon over the tomato sauce.

8 Microwave two plates at a time on HIGH for 1 minute until heated through. Garnish with fresh basil and serve hot with wholemeal bread.

Piquant Chicken Livers with Fresh Pears

Serves 6
202 calories per serving

450 g (1 lb) chicken livers, trimmed

2 small ripe pears

15 ml (1 tbsp) lemon juice

15 ml (1 tbsp) brandy (optional)

45 ml (3 tbsp) polyunsaturated oil

30 ml (2 tbsp) apple juice

15 ml (1 tbsp) white wine vinegar

5 ml (1 level tsp) Dijon mustard

salt and pepper

1 small head curly endive, trimmed

25 g (1 oz) hazelnuts, roughly chopped, to garnish

The combination of sweet and savoury, and the contrast in texture, make this an unusual yet filling starter.

1 Cut the chicken livers into bite-sized pieces and place in a large shallow dish. Cover, leaving a gap to let steam escape, and microwave on HIGH for 7–8 minutes until the livers are just cooked, stirring once.

2 Meanwhile, core the pears and chop into bite-sized pieces. Place in a bowl, add the lemon juice and brandy, if using, and toss well to coat. Set aside.

3 Remove the livers from the dish with a slotted spoon and transfer to a medium bowl. Whisk the oil, apple juice, vinegar, mustard and salt and pepper to taste into the liquid remaining in the dish. Pour over the chicken livers and stir in the pears.

4 Cover, leaving a gap to let steam escape, and microwave on HIGH for 1–2 minutes or until *just* heated through.

5 To serve, arrange the endive on six individual serving plates and top with the liver mixture. Garnish with the chopped hazelnuts.

CHAPTER 4

Light Meals

Spicy Cheese and Nut Burgers

Makes 8
190 calories each

1 medium onion, skinned and finely chopped

2 medium carrots, scrubbed and grated

2.5 ml ($\frac{1}{2}$ level tsp) cumin seeds

2.5 ml ($\frac{1}{2}$ level tsp) coriander seeds, finely crushed

100 g (4 oz) Edam cheese, grated

50 g (2 oz) walnuts, finely chopped

50 g (2 oz) blanched almonds, finely chopped

100 g (4 oz) wholemeal breadcrumbs

salt and pepper

1 egg, beaten

15 ml (1 tbsp) polyunsaturated oil

lemon wedges, to garnish

For the salad

$\frac{1}{2}$ cucumber

300 ml ($\frac{1}{2}$ pint) low-fat natural yogurt

15 ml (1 tbsp) chopped fresh mint

A natural yogurt and cucumber salad should be served with these burgers to provide a refreshing accompaniment which contrasts well with the richness of the spicy nut mixture.

1 To make the salad, coarsely grate the cucumber. Put in a sieve and squeeze out as much of the water as possible. Put the yogurt in a bowl and stir in the cucumber, mint and salt and pepper to taste. Chill while making the burgers.

2 Put the onion and carrots in a medium bowl with 15 ml (1 tbsp) water. Cover, leaving a gap to let steam escape, and microwave on HIGH for 5–7 minutes until the vegetables have softened, stirring occasionally.

3 Stir in the cumin and coriander seeds and microwave on HIGH for 1 minute, stirring once. Remove and set aside.

4 Heat a large browning dish on HIGH for 5–8 minutes or according to manufacturer's instructions.

5 Meanwhile, stir the cheese, walnuts, almonds and breadcrumbs into the vegetables. Season with pepper to taste. Stir in the egg to bind the mixture together. Divide the mixture into eight and shape into burgers.

6 When the browning dish is hot, add the oil and microwave on HIGH for 30 seconds.

7 Carefully add the burgers and microwave on HIGH for 2 minutes, then turn them over and microwave on HIGH for a further 2 minutes or until browned. Serve hot or cold, garnished with lemon wedges and the yogurt and cucumber salad.

Mushroom and Lentil Croquettes

Makes 6
140 calories each

45 ml (3 tbsp) polyunsaturated oil

225 g (8 oz) button mushrooms, roughly chopped

Lentils are the only pulses that do not need to be soaked before cooking. The most popular red lentils are used in this recipe and they are quick and easy to use.

1 Put 15 ml (1 tbsp) of the oil, the mushrooms, onion and garlic in a large bowl. Microwave on HIGH for

1 medium onion, skinned and
finely chopped

1 garlic clove, skinned and
crushed

5 ml (1 level tsp) paprika

125 g (4 oz) split red lentils

5 ml (1 tsp) lemon juice

1 egg, beaten

45 ml (3 tbsp) chopped fresh
parsley

salt and pepper

lemon wedges, to garnish

5–6 minutes until softened, stirring occasionally.

2 Stir in the paprika and microwave on HIGH for
1 minute, stirring once.

3 Add the lentils, lemon juice and 300 ml ($\frac{1}{2}$ pint)
boiling water. Mix well and microwave on HIGH
for 15 minutes until the lentils are tender and all the
water has been absorbed, stirring occasionally. Leave
to cool for a few minutes.

4 Add the egg and parsley to the lentils and beat until
the mixture is bound together. Season with salt and
pepper to taste. Leave until cold, then chill for about
1 hour to firm the mixture.

5 Divide the mixture into six and shape into
triangular croquettes. Chill again for 30 minutes.

6 Heat a large browning dish on HIGH for
5 minutes or according to manufacturer's
instructions. When the browning dish is hot, add the
remaining oil and microwave on HIGH for
30 seconds.

7 Carefully add the croquettes and microwave on
HIGH for $1\frac{1}{2}$–2 minutes. Turn them over and
microwave on HIGH for a further $1\frac{1}{2}$–2 minutes until
browned. Serve hot, garnished with lemon wedges.

Piperade

Serves 4
125 calories per serving

1 large onion, skinned and very
thinly sliced

1 garlic clove, skinned and
crushed (optional)

1 large red pepper, seeded and
very thinly sliced

1 large green pepper, seeded
and very thinly sliced

350 g (12 oz) tomatoes,
skinned and roughly chopped

4 eggs, beaten

15 ml (1 tbsp) chopped fresh
parsley

salt and pepper

Cook the vegetables until all the liquid has
evaporated, before adding the eggs, otherwise the
dish will separate and be too wet.

1 Put the onion, garlic, peppers and tomatoes in a
large shallow dish and mix together. Microwave on
HIGH for 10–15 minutes or until softened, stirring
occasionally.

2 Beat the eggs and parsley together and stir into the
vegetables. Season with salt and pepper to taste and
microwave on HIGH for 2–3 minutes, until the eggs
are very lightly set, stirring frequently. Serve
immediately with wholemeal toast.

Cheese and Herb Jacket Potatoes

Serves 2
200 calories per serving

two 175 g (6 oz) old potatoes

225 g (8 oz) fromage frais

30 ml (2 tbsp) chopped fresh mixed herbs

freshly grated nutmeg

salt and pepper

5 ml (1 level tsp) grated fresh Parmesan cheese

chopped fresh herbs, to garnish

Fromage frais is a soft cheese made from skimmed milk which means it is low in both fat and calories. Make sure that you buy the kind without added cream.

1 Wash the potatoes and prick all over with a fork. Place on absorbent kitchen paper. Microwave on HIGH for 6–8 minutes or until soft. Turn over once during cooking.

2 Cut the potatoes in half lengthways and scoop out the flesh with a teaspoon into a bowl. Leave a thin shell and be careful not to puncture the skin.

3 Mash the potato flesh with the cheese and herbs and season with nutmeg, salt and pepper to taste.

4 Pile the mixture back into the potato shells and arrange on an ovenproof serving plate. Microwave on HIGH for 1–2 minutes until heated through. Sprinkle with the Parmesan cheese and chopped fresh herbs to garnish.

Avocado, Prawn and Potato Salad

Serves 4
260 calories per serving

350 g (12 oz) small new potatoes, scrubbed and quartered

1 small ripe avocado

150 ml ($\frac{1}{4}$ pint) low-fat natural yogurt

15 ml (1 tbsp) lemon juice

5 ml (1 level tsp) wholegrain mustard

salt and pepper

225 g (8 oz) peeled prawns

4 large radishes, trimmed and thinly sliced

2 spring onions, trimmed and thinly sliced

few lettuce leaves, to garnish

Although avocados are high in fat, it is mostly the unsaturated type. Avocados contain large amounts of B vitamins and, when seasoned and mixed with yogurt, make a nutritious dressing.

1 Put the potatoes into a medium bowl with 30 ml (2 tbsp) water. Cover, leaving a gap to let steam escape, and microwave on HIGH for 7–8 minutes or until tender, stirring occasionally.

2 Meanwhile, cut the avocado in half and mash half of the flesh with the yogurt, lemon juice, mustard and salt and pepper to taste.

3 Pour the dressing over the potatoes and toss together with the prawns. Cut the remaining avocado into cubes and mix into the salad with the radishes and spring onions.

4 Serve while still slightly warm, garnished with a few lettuce leaves.

Granary Bread Pizzas

Serves 4
174 calories per serving

397 g (14 oz) can chopped tomatoes

15 ml (1 level tbsp) tomato purée

1 garlic clove, skinned and crushed

salt and pepper

1 wholemeal or granary stick, about 40.5 cm (16 inches) long

50 g (2 oz) mushrooms, thinly sliced

1 medium onion, skinned and thinly sliced

1 green pepper, seeded and cut into thin rings

50 g (2 oz) Mozzarella cheese, grated

5 ml (1 level tsp) dried oregano

Try making these bread-based pizzas instead of simply heating up a commercially prepared one; they are much more nutritious and just as quick and easy.

1 Put the chopped tomatoes with their juice, tomato purée, garlic and salt and pepper to taste in a medium bowl. Microwave on HIGH for 5 minutes or until boiling and slightly reduced.

2 Meanwhile, cut the bread stick in half, then cut each half in half again horizontally to make four pizza bases.

3 Spoon the tomato sauce evenly over the bread and arrange the mushrooms, onion and green pepper on top. Sprinkle with the cheese and oregano.

4 Arrange the pizzas on two ovenproof serving plates and microwave, one plate at a time, on HIGH for 2–3 minutes or until hot. Serve immediately with a green salad.

Pitta Bread with Chicken and Beansprouts

Serves 2
303 calories per serving

1 red pepper, seeded and cut into thin strips

1 small onion, skinned and thinly sliced

1 medium carrot, scrubbed and grated

100 g (4 oz) cooked chicken, cut into strips

50 g (2 oz) beansprouts

15 ml (1 tbsp) shoyu sauce

5 ml (1 tsp) clear honey

5 ml (1 level tsp) Dijon mustard

2 wholemeal pitta breads

You can substitute cooked peeled prawns or lean cooked ham for the chicken in this dish if you prefer.

1 Put all the ingredients except the pitta bread into a large bowl, and mix well. Cover, leaving a gap to let steam escape, and microwave on HIGH for 5 minutes, or until the vegetables are just tender, stirring once. Set aside.

2 Place the pitta breads on absorbent kitchen paper and microwave on HIGH for 30 seconds or until just warm.

3 Split and fill the pitta breads with the beansprout and chicken mixture. Serve immediately.

SLIM AND HEALTHY MICROWAVE COOKERY

Hummus-filled Jacket Potatoes

Serves 2
405 calories per serving

2 large potatoes, each weighing about 200 g (7 oz)

397 g (14 oz) can cooked chick peas, drained and rinsed

1–2 garlic cloves, skinned and crushed

juice of 1 lemon

15 ml (1 tbsp) tahini

salt and pepper

cayenne pepper

ground cumin

60 ml (4 tbsp) low-fat natural yogurt

chopped fresh parsley, to garnish

Hummus is a classic recipe from the Middle East, made basically from chick peas, tahini and garlic. Tahini is a sesame-seed paste and is widely available from health food shops. This combination of chick peas and sesame seeds is high in fibre, protein and B vitamins.

1 Scrub the potatoes and pat dry. Prick each potato several times with a fork and place on absorbent kitchen paper. Microwave on HIGH for 7–10 minutes or until soft, turning over once halfway through cooking.

2 Meanwhile, make the hummus. Put the chick peas, garlic and lemon juice in a blender or food processor and purée until the chick peas are well mashed.

3 Add the tahini and season with salt, pepper, cayenne pepper and ground cumin to taste. Purée until smooth. Add the yogurt and work for a further few seconds until well mixed.

4 To serve, cut the potatoes in half lengthways and arrange on two serving plates. Spoon over the hummus, sprinkle with parsley and serve immediately with a mixed salad.

Poached Eggs with Mushroom Purée

Serves 2
205 calories per serving

225 g (8 oz) dark, flat mushrooms, thinly sliced

1 small onion, skinned and thinly sliced

30 ml (2 tbsp) chopped fresh parsley

30 ml (2 tbsp) Greek strained yogurt

salt and pepper

freshly grated nutmeg

2.5 ml (½ tsp) vinegar

2 eggs

2 slices of wholemeal toast

This delicious snack, served on toast, would also make a good addition to a Sunday brunch.

1 Put the mushrooms into a large bowl with the onion. Cover, leaving a gap to let steam escape, and microwave on HIGH for 3 minutes. Uncover and microwave on HIGH for a further 4 minutes.

2 Transfer the mushroom mixture to a blender or food processor with the parsley and yogurt and work until smooth. Season with salt, pepper and nutmeg to taste. Set aside.

3 Pour 450 ml (¾ pint) boiling water and the vinegar into a large shallow dish. Microwave on HIGH for 1–2 minutes until the water returns to the boil.

4 Carefully break each egg on to a saucer, prick the yolk with a fine skewer or the point of a sharp knife and slide one at a time into the water.

5 Cover, leaving a gap to let steam escape, and microwave on HIGH for 1 minute. Leave to stand for 1–2 minutes to allow the eggs to set.

6 Cover the mushroom purée, leaving a gap to let steam escape, and microwave on HIGH for 1 minute to heat through.

7 To serve, spoon the purée on to the toast. Using a slotted spoon, transfer the eggs on top of the purée. Serve immediately.

Note: To poach 4 eggs, use 600 ml (1 pint) boiling water with 5 ml (1 tsp) vinegar and proceed as above. After adding the eggs, cover and cook for $1\frac{1}{2}$–2 minutes.

Cauliflower with Cheese and Mushrooms

Serves 4
155 calories per serving

900 g (2 lb) cauliflower, trimmed and broken into large florets

150 ml ($\frac{1}{4}$ pint) boiling vegetable stock

1 green pepper, seeded and cut into thin strips

30 ml (2 level tbsp) fine oatmeal

3 large tomatoes, roughly chopped

175 g (6 oz) mushrooms, sliced

100 g (4 oz) Edam cheese, grated

salt and pepper

chopped fresh parsley, to garnish

In this tempting recipe, all of the nutrients are retained because the cooking liquid is used to make the sauce.

1 Put the cauliflower into a large bowl with the stock. Cover, leaving a gap to let steam escape, and microwave on HIGH for 8–10 minutes or until just tender, stirring once.

2 Drain the cauliflower and transfer to an ovenproof serving dish. Set aside.

3 Stir the green pepper, oatmeal, tomatoes and mushrooms into the stock remaining in the dish and mix well. Microwave on HIGH for 7–8 minutes until the pepper is softened and the sauce is slightly thickened, stirring once. Stir in half of the cheese and season with salt and pepper to taste.

4 Pour the sauce over the cauliflower and sprinkle with the remaining cheese. Microwave on HIGH for 2–3 minutes or until the cheese is melted. Serve immediately, garnished with parsley.

Chicken Tikka

Serves 4
220 calories per serving

4 chicken breast fillets, skinned

juice of ½ lemon

2.5 cm (1 inch) piece fresh root ginger, peeled and finely grated

1 green chilli, seeded and chopped

2 garlic cloves, skinned and crushed

5 ml (1 level tsp) garam masala

5 ml (1 level tsp) paprika

5 ml (1 level tsp) ground turmeric

5 ml (1 level tsp) ground cumin

5 ml (1 level tsp) ground coriander

30 ml (2 tbsp) chopped fresh coriander

150 ml (¼ pint) low-fat natural yogurt

lemon wedges, to garnish

For the salad

2 medium red or Spanish onions, skinned

½ cucumber

1 small green pepper, seeded

30 ml (2 tbsp) chopped fresh coriander

juice of ½ lemon

5 ml (1 tsp) olive oil

salt and pepper

This Indian speciality, adapted here for the microwave, produces a wonderfully moist and spicy result. Accompanied by an onion, cucumber and pepper salad, it is equally good served hot or cold.

1 Cut the chicken into 2.5 cm (1 inch) cubes and place in a shallow dish. Put the lemon juice, ginger, chilli, garlic, garam masala, paprika, turmeric, cumin, ground coriander, the fresh coriander and yogurt in a blender or food processor and work until smooth.

2 Pour over the chicken, cover and leave to marinate in the refrigerator for at least 6 hours.

3 To make the salad, halve the onion and slice very thinly. Cut the cucumber into thin slices, then cut each slice crossways to make very thin strips. Cut the green pepper into very thin slices.

4 Mix the onion, cucumber and pepper together and sprinkle with the fresh coriander. Mix the lemon juice with the oil, pour over the salad and toss together until well mixed. Season with salt and pepper to taste, cover and leave to marinate in the refrigerator until ready to serve.

5 When ready to serve, thread the chicken on to eight wooden skewers and arrange in a single layer in a shallow dish. Cover loosely with absorbent kitchen paper and microwave on HIGH for 6–7 minutes or until tender, turning and basting with the marinade once during cooking. Garnish with lemon wedges, then serve the chicken tikka with the salad and warm wholemeal pitta bread.

AVOCADO, PRAWN AND POTATO SALAD (PAGE 44)

Tuna Pizza

Serves 2
570 calories per serving

100 g (4 oz) wholemeal self-raising flour

25 g (1 oz) white self-raising flour

salt and pepper

90–105 ml (6–7 tbsp) skimmed milk

15 ml (1 tbsp) polyunsaturated oil

198 g (7 oz) can tuna fish in brine, drained and flaked

5 ml (1 tsp) chopped fresh oregano (optional)

3 tomatoes, sliced

1 small onion, skinned and thinly sliced

100 g (4 oz) Mozzarella cheese, coarsely grated

3 green olives, halved

Canned fish is a store cupboard staple—high in vitamin D, it forms part of many quick, nutritious meals. Buy tuna fish canned in brine to avoid the added fat of fish canned in oil.

1 Put the flour and a pinch of salt in a bowl, make a well in the centre and add the milk. Gradually beat in the milk to form a soft dough.

2 Heat a large browning dish on HIGH for 5–8 minutes or according to manufacturer's instructions.

3 Meanwhile, turn the dough out on a lightly floured work surface and knead until smooth. Roll out to a 20.5 cm (8 inch) round. Brush generously with some of the oil.

4 Using a fish slice, quickly put the pizza dough into the browning dish, oiled side down, and microwave on HIGH for 2–3 minutes or until the surface of the dough looks slightly dry.

5 Brush with more oil and turn over. Microwave on HIGH for 1–2 minutes until cooked.

6 Arrange the tuna evenly over the pizza base, right to the edges. Sprinkle with the oregano if using then scatter the tomatoes, onion and Mozzarella on top. Place the olives over the top of the cheese and season with pepper to taste.

7 Microwave on HIGH for 3–4 minutes or until the cheese has melted. Serve hot with a salad.

BUCKWHEAT SPAGHETTI WITH SMOKED SALMON (PAGE 51)

CHAPTER 5

Fish Main Courses

Mackerel with Celery and Oatmeal

Serves 4
422 calories per serving

2 mackerel, each weighing about 450 g (1 lb), cleaned

4 celery sticks, trimmed and roughly chopped

25 g (1 oz) fresh wholemeal breadcrumbs

50 g (2 oz) coarse oatmeal

25 g (1 oz) seedless raisins, chopped

finely grated rind and juice of ½ lemon

salt and pepper

1 egg, size 6

Although mackerel is an oily fish, a high proportion of its fat is polyunsaturated. The topping for these mackerel fillets comprises celery, wholemeal breadcrumbs, oatmeal and raisins—all good sources of fibre.

1 Cut the head and tail off the fish and split open along the underside. Place on a board, flesh side down, and press firmly along the backbone to release it. Ease out the bone and cut into two fillets. Rinse and dry the fish. Make a few shallow cuts in the skin.

2 Place the fillets in a single layer in a shallow dish, skin side down.

3 Mix the celery with the breadcrumbs, oatmeal, raisins and lemon rind and juice. Season with salt and pepper to taste and stir in the egg to bind the mixture together.

4 Pile the filling on to the mackerel spreading it evenly along the flesh. Cover, leaving a gap to let steam escape, and microwave on HIGH for about 10 minutes until the fish is tender. Serve with a green salad.

Buckwheat Spaghetti with Smoked Salmon

Serves 3
346 calories per serving

225 g (8 oz) buckwheat spaghetti

75 g (3 oz) smoked salmon trimmings

finely grated rind and juice of ½ small lemon

75 ml (3 fl oz) buttermilk

30 ml (2 tbsp) snipped fresh chives

1 egg, beaten

pepper

fresh chives, to garnish

Buckwheat spaghetti is made from the roasted seeds of a plant native to China. It is a useful source of protein, minerals and vitamin B and makes a delicious alternative to wholemeal pasta.

1 Break the spaghetti in half and put into a large bowl. Pour over 1.1 litres (2 pints) boiling water and stir. Cover, leaving a gap to let steam escape, and microwave on HIGH for 5–6 minutes until almost tender. Leave to stand, covered, while making the sauce. Do not drain.

2 Cut the salmon into neat pieces and put into an ovenproof serving bowl with the remaining ingredients and pepper to taste. Microwave on HIGH for 1 minute or until slightly warmed, stirring once.

3 Drain the pasta and rinse with boiling water. Quickly stir into the sauce and toss together to mix. Garnish with chives and serve immediately with a mixed salad.

Mediterranean Baked Mackerel

Serves 4
375 calories per serving

2 mackerel, each weighing about 450 g (1 lb), cleaned and heads removed

salt and pepper

5 ml (1 level tsp) dried oregano

5 ml (1 level tsp) dried marjoram

5 ml (1 level tsp) dried thyme

1 large onion, skinned and thinly sliced

2 garlic cloves, skinned and crushed

225 g (8 oz) tomatoes, coarsely chopped

1 small green pepper, seeded and cut into thin strips

50 g (2 oz) black olives

30 ml (2 tbsp) chopped fresh parsley

150 ml ($\frac{1}{4}$ pint) dry white wine

Oily fish such as mackerel are a good source of vitamins A and D and are also rich in polyunsaturated fat. You should aim to eat at least one oily fish meal a week. In this recipe, whole mackerel are cooked with herbs, tomatoes, onion, green pepper and white wine.

1 Season the mackerel with salt and pepper to taste and sprinkle the insides with half of the herbs.

2 Sprinkle the remaining herbs in the base of a shallow dish, large enough to take the fish in a single layer. Sprinkle half of the onion on top of the herbs and arrange the fish on top.

3 Sprinkle with the remaining ingredients and pour over the wine.

4 Cover, leaving a gap to let steam escape, and microwave on HIGH for 12–13 minutes or until the fish is very tender. Leave to stand for 5 minutes, then serve with new potatoes cooked in their skins.

Peppered Mackerel and Sesame Fish Cakes

Makes 6
230 calories per serving

2 medium potatoes, each weighing about 175 g (6 oz)

2 smoked mackerel fillets with crushed black peppercorns, total weight about 275 g (10 oz)

finely grated rind and juice of 1 large lemon

1 egg, beaten

40 g (1$\frac{1}{2}$ oz) sesame seeds

15 ml (1 tbsp) polyunsaturated oil

lemon wedges, to garnish

Rich in protein, calcium and B vitamins, the sesame seeds are used to coat the fish cakes in this recipe. Other fish such as cod or haddock can be used but they should be cooked first.

1 Wash the potatoes and prick all over with a fork. Place on absorbent kitchen paper. Microwave on HIGH for 8–10 minutes or until soft, turning over halfway through cooking.

2 Meanwhile, flake the mackerel, discarding the skin and any bones. Put in a bowl and mix with the lemon rind and juice.

3 When the potatoes are cooked, cut in half, scoop out the flesh and mash until smooth. Stir into the mackerel mixture and beat thoroughly together. Stir in half of the egg to bind together.

4 Heat a browning dish on HIGH for 5–8 minutes or according to manufacturer's instructions.

5 Meanwhile, shape the mixture into six small cake shapes about 1 cm ($\frac{1}{2}$ inch) thick. Brush lightly with the remaining beaten egg and coat in the sesame seeds.

6 Pour the oil into the browning dish, then quickly add the fish cakes. Microwave on HIGH for 2 minutes, then turn over and microwave on HIGH for a further 2 minutes. Garnish and serve hot.

Salmon with Courgettes and Mushrooms

Serves 2
240 calories per serving

225 g (8 oz) courgettes

125 g (4 oz) carrots, scrubbed

125 g (4 oz) mushrooms, sliced

30 ml (2 tbsp) chopped fresh parsley

finely grated rind and juice of 1 lime

salt and pepper

2 salmon steaks or cutlets, each weighing about 175 g (6 oz)

In this recipe, it is important to choose fish steaks of a similar thickness to ensure even cooking. If they are less than 2 cm ($\frac{3}{4}$ inch) thick, reduce the cooking time slightly. The vegetables in this recipe remain quite crunchy—slice them more thinly if you prefer a softer texture.

1 Cut the courgettes and carrots into 0.5 cm ($\frac{1}{4}$ inch) slices.

2 Put the courgettes, carrots and mushrooms in a large shallow dish with the parsley, lime rind and salt and pepper to taste. Pour over the lime juice. Place the fish side by side on top of the vegetables.

3 Cover, leaving a gap to let steam escape, and microwave on HIGH for 6 minutes until the fish is tender. Serve hot.

Plaice Steamed with Herbs

Serves 2
225 calories per serving

3 large tomatoes, roughly chopped

1 spring onion, trimmed and finely chopped

4 plaice fillets, total weight about 450 g (1 lb), skinned

30 ml (2 tbsp) chopped mixed herbs, such as parsley, dill, tarragon

10 ml (2 tsp) lemon juice

salt and pepper

This is an excellent method of cooking plaice in the microwave and works equally well with other fish fillets too.

1 Sprinkle the tomatoes and spring onion on a large ovenproof serving plate. Arrange the plaice fillets in a single layer on top.

2 Sprinkle with the herbs and lemon juice and season with salt and pepper to taste.

3 Cover, leaving a gap to let steam escape, and microwave on HIGH for 5–6 minutes or until tender. Serve immediately with a green vegetable.

Poached Salmon with Watercress Sauce

Serves 2
310 calories per serving

2 salmon steaks, each weighing about 175 g (6 oz)

2 bay leaves

30 ml (2 tbsp) dry white wine

½ bunch of watercress, trimmed and tough stalks discarded

150 ml (¼ pint) smetana

5 ml (1 tsp) lemon juice

salt and pepper

Vitamin- and mineral-packed watercress is puréed here to provide a delicate green sauce which complements the pink of the salmon.

1 Put the salmon steaks into a shallow dish large enough to hold them in a single layer, arranging the thickest parts towards the outside of the dish. Put a bay leaf on top of each steak and pour over the wine. Cover, leaving a gap to let steam escape, and microwave on HIGH for 4–5 minutes or until tender.

2 Meanwhile, roughly chop the watercress, reserving about a handful of the smallest leaves for the garnish. Put the chopped watercress, smetana and lemon juice in a blender or food processor and work until very finely chopped.

3 Arrange the salmon steaks on two warmed serving plates. Microwave the cooking liquid remaining in the dish, uncovered, on HIGH for 1 minute or until boiling.

4 Discard the bay leaves, then gradually pour the cooking liquid into the watercress dressing in the blender or food processor and work until just mixed together. Season with salt and pepper to taste.

5 Pour a little of the sauce over the salmon steaks and sprinkle with the reserved watercress leaves. Serve immediately with the remaining sauce. Alternatively, leave to cool and serve cold.

Smoked Haddock Pilaff

Serves 3–4
502–376 calories per serving

225 g (8 oz) long-grain brown rice

450 ml (¾ pint) boiling fish stock

pepper

450 g (1 lb) tomatoes

450 g (1 lb) leeks

450 g (1 lb) smoked haddock fillet

150 ml (¼ pint) dry white wine

The rice in this pilaff will still be slightly crunchy when taken from the microwave but it softens a little more as it absorbs liquid during the standing time.

1 Put the rice, stock and pepper to taste in a large bowl. Cover, leaving a gap to let steam escape, and microwave on HIGH for 30–35 minutes until tender, stirring once and adding a little extra water if necessary. Leave to stand for 5 minutes by which time all the water should be absorbed.

2 Meanwhile, skin and quarter the tomatoes. Slice the leeks into 1 cm (½ inch) thick pieces, wash well then drain. Skin the fish and divide into large chunks.

3 Stir the tomatoes, leeks, fish and wine into the cooked rice, making sure that most of the rice is under liquid. Re-cover and microwave on HIGH for 15 minutes.

4 Leave to stand for about 10 minutes. Uncover and stir the rice with a fork. Serve with a mixed salad.

Sardines with Lemon and Parsley

Serves 4
360 calories per serving

900 g (2 lb) (at least 12) fresh or frozen sardines, cleaned if wished

15 ml (1 tbsp) olive oil

grated rind and juice of 1 lemon

60 ml (4 tbsp) chopped fresh parsley

pepper

lemon wedges, to garnish

Sardines, although oily fish, contain polyunsaturated fats: they are a very healthy food, being a good source of protein, iodine and vitamins A and D.

1 Wash the sardines well and scrape off the scales. Using a sharp knife, make two diagonal slashes on each side of the fish.

2 Put the oil in a shallow dish large enough to hold the fish in a single layer. Microwave on HIGH for 30 seconds. Arrange the fish in the dish and microwave on HIGH for 3 minutes.

3 Turn the fish over and sprinkle with the lemon rind and juice, parsley and pepper to taste. Microwave on HIGH for a further 3 minutes until the fish are tender. Serve garnished with lemon wedges.

Fish en Papillote

Serves 2
245 calories per serving

2 red mullet, each weighing about 175 g (6 oz), cleaned and scaled

salt and pepper

½ small onion, skinned and thinly sliced

2 parsley sprigs

2 bay leaves

2 slices of lemon

This simple method of cooking fish in greaseproof paper parcels works just as well with any other small, whole fish.

1 Slash the fish on each side using a sharp knife. Season the insides with salt and pepper to taste. Use the onion, parsley, bay leaves and lemon slices to stuff the fish.

2 Cut two 30.5 cm (12 inch) squares of greaseproof paper. Place a fish on each piece and fold it to make a neat parcel, twisting the ends together to seal. Place on a large flat plate.

3 Microwave on HIGH for 3–4 minutes or until the fish is tender. Serve the fish in their parcels.

Trout with Almonds and Cumin Sauce

Serves 2
330 calories per serving

15 g (½ oz) flaked almonds

2 medium trout, cleaned and heads removed

salt and pepper

finely grated rind and juice of ½ lemon

2.5 ml (½ level tsp) cumin seeds, finely crushed

50 ml (2 fl oz) dry white wine

75 ml (3 fl oz) smetana

25 g (1 oz) ground almonds

Both flaked and ground almonds, high in potassium, calcium and iron, are used in this dish. The ground almonds make a nutritious thickening agent.

1 Put the flaked almonds on a large flat plate. Microwave on HIGH for 6–8 minutes or until lightly browned, stirring occasionally. Set aside.

2 Place the trout in a shallow dish and season inside and out with salt and pepper to taste. Sprinkle with the lemon rind and pour over the lemon juice. Cover, leaving a gap to let steam escape, and microwave on HIGH for 3 minutes. Turn the fish over, re-cover and microwave on HIGH for 2–3 minutes or until the fish is tender.

3 Transfer the fish to a warmed serving dish and keep hot.

4 Stir the remaining ingredients into the liquid left in the dish and mix together. Microwave on HIGH for 3–4 minutes or until slightly thickened, stirring occasionally. Season with salt and pepper to taste. Pour over the trout and garnish with the flaked almonds. Serve immediately.

Smoked Trout and Pasta Salad

Serves 4–6
277–185 calories per serving

175 g (6 oz) wholemeal pasta shapes

2 smoked trout, skinned and filleted

15 ml (1 tbsp) olive oil

5 ml (1 level tsp) mild mustard

10 ml (2 level tsp) tomato purée

45 ml (3 tbsp) low-fat natural yogurt

15 ml (1 tbsp) chopped fresh dill (optional)

pepper

Smoked trout is widely available in delicatessens or on the delicatessen counter in larger supermarkets. Combined with pasta and a piquant yogurt dressing, this smoked trout dish provides a tangy, satisfying meal.

1 Put the pasta in a large bowl. Pour over 900 ml (1½ pints) boiling water and stir. Cover, leaving a gap to let steam escape, and microwave on HIGH for 8–10 minutes or until just tender. Leave to stand, covered. Do not drain.

2 Meanwhile, flake the fish and turn into a serving dish.

3 Mix the oil with the mustard and tomato purée. Gradually stir in the yogurt and dill, if using. Season with pepper to taste.

OPPOSITE: MIXED SEAFOOD WITH SAFFRON SAUCE (PAGE 60)
OVERLEAF: FISH EN PAPILLOTE (PAGE 55)

100 g (4 oz) green beans, trimmed and cut in half

4 tomatoes, cut into small wedges

50 g (2 oz) black olives, halved

4 Put the beans on an ovenproof plate with 30 ml (2 tbsp) water. Cover, leaving a gap to let steam escape, and microwave on HIGH for 3–4 minutes or until just tender. Drain and add to the smoked trout.

5 Drain the pasta, return to the bowl and pour on the dressing. Toss thoroughly together then mix with the beans and smoked trout. Add the tomatoes and olives and mix together. Serve immediately with chunks of wholemeal bread.

Red Mullet with Hot Red Pepper Sauce

Serves 4
255 calories per serving

1 large red pepper

7.5 ml (1½ tsp) sweet chilli sauce

75 ml (5 tbsp) vegetable stock

salt and pepper

four 175 g (6 oz) red mullet, cleaned and scaled

lemon or lime wedges, to garnish

Be sure to use sweet or mild chilli sauce for this recipe or the result will be inedible even for the strongest palate!

1 Place the pepper in a large bowl with 30 ml (2 tbsp) water. Cover, leaving a gap to let steam escape, and microwave on HIGH for 10–12 minutes until very soft.

2 Plunge the pepper into cold water for 1 minute. Drain well, remove the seeds and peel off the skin.

3 Place the pepper in a blender or food processor with the chilli sauce and stock and work until smooth. Season with salt and pepper to taste.

4 Slash the fish on each side and arrange in a large flat dish. Add 45 ml (3 tbsp) water. Cover, leaving a gap to let steam escape, and microwave on HIGH for 4–5 minutes or until tender, turning the fish over half way through cooking. Allow to stand while reheating the sauce.

5 Put the sauce in a medium bowl. Cover, leaving a gap to let steam escape, and microwave on HIGH for 1–2 minutes until heated through.

6 To serve, place a fish on four warmed serving plates and spoon over the sauce. Garnish with lemon or lime wedges.

Opposite: Tofu and bean burgers (page 70)
Previous page: Fish en papillote (page 55)

Medallions of Monkfish with Lime

Serves 4
172 calories per serving

700 g (1½ lb) monkfish,
skinned

1 lime

15 ml (1 tbsp) olive oil

75 ml (3 fl oz) dry white wine

salt and pepper

30 ml (2 tbsp) Greek strained
yogurt

lime wedges, to garnish

Vitamin C-rich limes have a much more distinctive flavour than lemons. Here they provide a lovely fresh, sharp tasting sauce.

1 Cut the fish down each side of the central bone. Then cut into 5 cm (2 inch) slices. Place between two sheets of greaseproof paper and flatten each slice slightly using a rolling pin, to make medallions about 0.5 cm (¼ inch) thick.

2 Heat a large browning dish on HIGH for 5–8 minutes or according to manufacturer's instructions.

3 Meanwhile, peel the rind from the lime, using a potato peeler or very sharp knife, and cut into very thin strips. Squeeze the juice.

4 Add the oil to the browning dish, then quickly add the monkfish. Microwave on HIGH for 1 minute, then turn over and microwave on HIGH for 1 minute or until the fish is just cooked. Transfer to a warmed serving dish.

5 Add the lime zest and juice, the wine and salt and pepper to taste to the browning dish. Mix together and microwave on HIGH for 4–5 minutes until reduced.

6 Stir in the yogurt, pour over the fish and serve immediately garnished with lime wedges.

Monkfish with Fennel and Lettuce

Serves 4
180 calories per serving

700 g (1½ lb) monkfish fillet,
skinned

½ small fennel head, trimmed
and very finely chopped

1 small onion, skinned and
very finely chopped

1 ripe pear, peeled and finely
chopped

Cooking lettuce briefly in the microwave preserves its pale green colour, and it is used here to provide an unusual contrast to the creamy white of the monkfish. You may substitute the monkfish with another firmly fleshed white fish such as cod, but the appearance will not be as good because it tends to break up during cooking.

1 Cut the fish into 4 cm (1½ inch) cubes and put into a large shallow dish.

75 g (3 oz) low-fat soft cheese

30 ml (2 tbsp) dry vermouth

salt and pepper

15 ml (1 tbsp) chopped fresh tarragon or 5 ml (1 level tsp) dried

15 ml (1 tbsp) chopped fennel fronds

½ Webbs Wonder or Cos lettuce, finely shredded

2 Mix the fennel, onion, pear, cheese and vermouth together and season with salt and pepper to taste. Pour over the fish and mix together. Microwave on HIGH for 4–5 minutes or until the fish is just cooked, stirring once.

3 Add the tarragon, fennel fronds and lettuce and mix thoroughly together. Microwave on HIGH for 1–2 minutes until the lettuce is heated through but not soggy. Serve immediately.

Mussels in White Wine

Serves 2
160 calories per serving

900 g (2 lb) fresh mussels

2 shallots, skinned and finely chopped

1 garlic clove, skinned and crushed

75 ml (5 tbsp) dry white wine

75 ml (5 tbsp) fish stock or water

30 ml (2 tbsp) chopped fresh parsley

salt and pepper

Mussels need careful preparation, but they are easy to cook in the microwave and remain succulent and tender.

1 To clean the mussels, put them in a sink or bowl and scrub thoroughly with a hard brush. Wash them in several changes of water.

2 Scrape off any 'beards' or tufts protruding from the shells, then leave the mussels to soak in a bowl of cold water for 20 minutes.

3 Drain the mussels, discard any damaged ones or any that do not close when tapped sharply with a knife.

4 Put the shallots, garlic, wine, stock and mussels into a large bowl. Cover, leaving a gap to let steam escape, and microwave on HIGH for 5–6 minutes or until all the mussels have opened, stirring once. Discard any mussels that have not opened.

5 Pile the mussels into a warmed serving dish. Stir the parsley into the liquid remaining in the bowl and season with salt and pepper to taste. Pour over the mussels and serve immediately accompanied by crusty bread.

Prawn and Sweetcorn Ragoût

Serves 4
202 calories per serving

1 green pepper, seeded and roughly chopped

1 medium onion, skinned and chopped

1 garlic clove, skinned and crushed

225 g (8 oz) sweetcorn kernels

450 g (1 lb) peeled prawns

15 ml (1 tbsp) chopped fresh dill or 5 ml (1 level tsp) dried

60 ml (4 tbsp) Greek strained yogurt

salt and pepper

Sweetcorn is an excellent source of fibre and, when accompanied by brown rice, provides the perfect basis for a high roughage meal.

1 Put the green pepper, onion, garlic and 15 ml (1 tbsp) water in an ovenproof serving dish. Cover, leaving a gap to let steam escape, and microwave on HIGH for 5 minutes until just softened but the pepper is still crisp.

2 Stir in the sweetcorn and prawns. Re-cover and microwave on HIGH for 3–5 minutes until the sweetcorn is tender.

3 Stir in the dill and yogurt and season with salt and pepper to taste. Serve with brown rice.

Mixed Seafood with Saffron Sauce

Serves 4
220 calories per serving

large pinch of saffron strands

50 ml (2 fl oz) dry white wine

strip of orange rind

1 bay leaf

450 g (1 lb) cod fillet, skinned

4 plaice quarter-cut fillets, each weighing about 50 g (2 oz), skinned

4 cooked unshelled jumbo prawns (optional)

15 ml (1 tbsp) Greek strained yogurt

salt and pepper

fresh herbs, to garnish

Vary the fish according to what is available, but always try to select an interesting combination of textures, colours and flavours.

1 Put the saffron, wine, orange rind and bay leaf in a small bowl. Microwave on HIGH for 2–3 minutes until boiling. Set aside to infuse while cooking the fish.

2 Cut the cod fillet into large chunks, and cut each plaice fillet in half. Arrange the fish and prawns, if using, in a single layer in a large shallow dish, placing the thinner pieces and the prawns towards the centre.

3 Pour over 30 ml (2 tbsp) of the infused sauce. Cover, leaving a gap to let steam escape, and microwave on HIGH for 5–6 minutes or until the fish is tender. Transfer the fish to four warmed serving plates.

4 Strain the remaining wine mixture into the cooking juices remaining in the dish, with the yogurt. Season with salt and pepper to taste. Microwave on HIGH for 1–2 minutes or until hot. Pour over the fish, garnish with herbs and serve immediately.

Scallops with Vegetables

Serves 4
240 calories per serving

4 spring onions, trimmed

4 medium carrots, scrubbed

3 medium courgettes, trimmed

12 large shelled scallops

15 ml (1 tbsp) polyunsaturated oil

1 garlic clove, skinned and finely chopped

1.25 ml ($\frac{1}{4}$ level tsp) grated fresh root ginger

1.25 ml ($\frac{1}{4}$ level tsp) five-spice powder

100 g (4 oz) beansprouts

grated rind of $\frac{1}{2}$ lemon

15 ml (1 tbsp) lemon juice

pepper

Stir-frying is a healthier cooking method than shallow or deep frying as it is extremely quick, retaining more nutrients and preventing the ingredients from soaking up too much oil.

1 Cut the spring onions into 5 cm (2 inch) lengths. Cut the carrots and courgettes into matchsticks, 5 cm (2 inches) long and 0.5 cm ($\frac{1}{4}$ inch) wide.

2 Cut the corals from the scallops and set aside. Remove the tough muscle which is found opposite the coral. Slice the scallops across the two discs. Put the oil in a large bowl and microwave on HIGH for 1–2 minutes or until hot.

3 Stir in the garlic, ginger and five-spice powder and microwave on HIGH for 1 minute. Stir in the scallops and microwave on HIGH for 3–4 minutes or until the scallops are opaque and tender, stirring once or twice during cooking. Remove from the bowl with a slotted spoon and set aside.

4 Add the spring onions, carrots, courgettes and beansprouts to the bowl. Microwave on HIGH for 6–7 minutes until the vegetables are tender, stirring every minute.

5 Return the scallops to the bowl, sprinkle over the lemon rind and juice and season with pepper to taste. Stir together, then microwave on HIGH for 2 minutes until heated through. Serve hot.

Marbled Fish Ring

Serves 6
200 calories per serving

200 g (7 oz) can tuna fish in brine

15 ml (1 level tbsp) tomato purée

15 ml (1 tbsp) lemon juice

2 egg whites

300 ml (½ pint) low-fat natural yogurt

pepper

700 g (1½ lb) white fish fillet, such as haddock, cod, whiting, skinned

100 g (4 oz) cottage cheese, drained

30 ml (2 tbsp) chopped fresh tarragon or 10 ml (2 level tsp) dried

15 ml (1 tbsp) chopped fresh dill or 5 ml (1 level tsp) dried

150 ml (¼ pint) smetana

salt

fresh dill, to garnish

This simple method of putting alternate spoonfuls of the two fish mixtures, one tuna and the other white fish, into a ring mould produces a most attractive result.

1 Drain the tuna and put into a blender or food processor with the tomato purée, lemon juice, one of the egg whites and 150 ml (¼ pint) of the yogurt. Work until smooth. Season with pepper to taste. Turn into a bowl and set aside.

2 Roughly chop the white fish fillet and put into the blender or food processor with the remaining yogurt, egg white, cottage cheese, half of the tarragon and half of the dill. Work until smooth, then season with pepper to taste.

3 Place alternate spoonfuls of the fish mixtures into a 1.1 litre (2 pint) ring mould, then draw a knife through the two mixtures in a spiral to make marbled effect. Level the surface.

4 Cover loosely with absorbent kitchen paper, then microwave on HIGH for 4–5 minutes or until the surface feels firm to the touch. Leave to cool, then chill in the refrigerator before serving.

5 When ready to serve, mix together the smetana and remaining tarragon and dill. Season with salt and pepper to taste.

6 Turn out the ring and wipe with absorbent kitchen paper to remove any liquid. Cut into thick slices, garnish with dill and serve with the sauce.

Marinated Sole with Citrus Fruits

Serves 4
182 calories per serving

6 sole fillets, each weighing about 100 g (4 oz), skinned

finely grated rind and juice of 1 lime

finely grated rind and juice of 1 lemon

finely grated rind and juice of 1 orange

Yellow, orange and green citrus fruit rinds make a very attractive contrast to the white fish. Substitute any other flat fish fillets for the sole if you prefer in this vitamin C-rich main course.

1 Cut the sole fillets in half widthways and place in a single layer in a large shallow dish. Mix the lime, lemon and orange rinds and juices with the oil, parsley and shallot. Season with salt and pepper to taste. Cover and leave to marinate for at least 3 hours.

15 ml (1 tbsp) olive oil

30 ml (2 tbsp) chopped fresh parsley

1 shallot, skinned and finely chopped

salt and pepper

lime, lemon and orange wedges, to garnish

2 Uncover the fish slightly, leaving a gap to let steam escape, and microwave on HIGH for 5–6 minutes or until tender.

3 Transfer the fish to a warmed serving dish and spoon over a little of the cooking liquid. Garnish with fruit wedges and serve immediately with new potatoes and a green vegetable.

Warm Squid and Celery Salad

Serves 4
170 calories per serving

450 g (1 lb) small squid

225 g (8 oz) new potatoes, scrubbed and cut into bite-sized chunks

45 ml (3 tbsp) lemon juice

grated rind of $\frac{1}{2}$ lemon

15 ml (1 tbsp) olive oil

10 ml (2 tsp) chopped fresh marjoram or parsley

salt and pepper

3 celery sticks, trimmed and finely sliced

1 medium yellow pepper, seeded and chopped

12 black olives, stoned

Squid, which are a good source of protein, have a slightly resilient texture which makes them a little chewy. This salad tastes best when eaten while still warm, but it can be served cold with equally good results. Try to use fresh herbs otherwise omit them.

1 To prepare the squid, remove the transparent quill or pen from the body pouch and discard.

2 Holding the body pouch in one hand, pull the head and tentacles away from the pouch. Cut through the head, just above the eyes to separate the tentacles from the rest of the innards. Discard eyes and ink sac.

3 Wash the tentacles under cold running water, rubbing with your fingers to remove the purplish skin. Cut the tentacles into small pieces.

4 Wash the body pouch under cold running water and rub off the purplish skin. Cut the body into thin rings. Set aside.

5 Place the potatoes in a large shallow dish and add 45 ml (3 tbsp) water. Cover, leaving a gap to let steam escape, and microwave on HIGH for about 5–7 minutes or until tender. Set aside.

6 Quarter fill a large bowl with boiling water and add the squid. Cover, leaving a gap to let steam escape, and microwave on HIGH for 2–3 minutes or until the squid *just* turns opaque. Drain the squid and potatoes and mix together in a large bowl.

7 Whisk together the lemon juice, rind, olive oil, marjoram or parsley and salt and pepper to taste. Pour over the potato and squid and mix well. Finally mix in the celery, yellow pepper and olives, toss well and serve while still warm.

Sole and Spinach Roulades

Serves 4
172 calories per serving

12 sole quarter-cut fillets, each weighing about 50 g (2 oz), skinned

5 ml (1 level tsp) fennel seeds, lightly crushed

salt and pepper

12 spinach or sorrel leaves, washed

15 ml (1 tbsp) dry white wine

45 ml (3 tbsp) Greek strained yogurt

pinch of ground turmeric

You will need to buy three whole sole and cut four fillets from each fish to make these pretty roulades.

1 Place the sole fillets, skin side up, on a chopping board, sprinkle with the fennel seeds and season with salt and pepper to taste. Lay a spinach leaf, vein side up, on top of each fillet. Roll up and secure with a wooden cocktail stick.

2 Arrange the fish in a circle around the edge of a large shallow dish and pour over the wine. Cover, leaving a gap to let steam escape, and microwave on HIGH for 6–7 minutes or until tender.

3 Using a slotted spoon, remove the fish from the cooking liquid to a warmed serving plate.

4 Gradually stir the yogurt and turmeric into the cooking liquid. Season and microwave on HIGH for 1–2 minutes until slightly thickened, stirring occasionally. Serve the roulades with the sauce.

Grey Mullet Stuffed with Garlic and Herbs

Serves 2–3
488–325 calories per serving

50 g (2 oz) hazelnuts

1 grey mullet, weighing about 700 g (1½ lb), cleaned and scaled

3 garlic cloves, skinned

finely grated rind and juice of 1 lemon

45 ml (3 tbsp) chopped fresh mixed herbs, such as parsley, basil, tarragon, chervil, mint, coriander

salt and pepper

15 ml (1 tbsp) olive oil

fresh herbs, to garnish

Grey mullet is a round fish which looks and tastes similar to sea bass. Here it is complemented by fresh mixed herbs and garlic.

1 Place the hazelnuts on an ovenproof plate. Microwave on HIGH for 3–4 minutes until lightly toasted. Set aside to cool.

2 Using a sharp knife, slash the fish three or four times on each side.

3 Put the hazelnuts, garlic, the lemon rind, half of the lemon juice and the herbs in a blender or food processor and work until a coarse paste. Season with salt and pepper. Spoon a little of the paste into the slashes and use the rest to stuff the fish.

4 Place the fish on a large ovenproof serving plate. Mix the remaining lemon juice with the oil and spoon over the fish. Season generously with pepper.

5 Cover, leaving a gap to let steam escape, and microwave on HIGH for 6–7 minutes or until tender. Leave to stand for 5 minutes, then garnish and serve.

BEAN GOULASH (PAGE 74)

CHAPTER 6

Vegetarian Main Courses

LAMB WITH AUBERGINE
AND MINT (PAGE 84)

Mixed Vegetables in Coconut Milk

Serves 6
230 calories per serving

50 g (2 oz) unsweetened desiccated coconut

300 ml (½ pint) soya milk

15 ml (1 tbsp) tahini

10 ml (2 tsp) olive oil

5 ml (1 level tsp) ground cumin

5 ml (1 level tsp) ground turmeric

450 g (1 lb) potatoes, scrubbed and cut into 0.5 cm (¼ inch) slices

225 g (8 oz) carrots, scrubbed and cut into 0.5 cm (¼ inch) slices

350 g (12 oz) parsnips, peeled and cut into 0.5 cm (¼ inch) slices

1 red pepper, seeded and sliced

225 g (8 oz) broccoli florets

salt and pepper

paprika

In this recipe, the coconut milk is made up using high protein soya milk and desiccated coconut.

1 Put the coconut and soya milk into a medium bowl and pour over 450 ml (¾ pint) boiling water. Stir in the tahini and set aside.

2 Put the oil, cumin and turmeric in a large bowl and mix together. Microwave on HIGH for 1 minute, stirring once.

3 Stir in the potatoes, carrots, parsnips and half of the coconut milk. Cover, leaving a gap to let steam escape, and microwave on HIGH for 13–15 minutes until the vegetables are tender, stirring occasionally.

4 Add the remaining coconut milk, red pepper and broccoli and season with salt, pepper and paprika to taste. Re-cover and microwave on HIGH for 2–3 minutes, until the pepper and broccoli are just tender. Serve hot.

Vegetable Biryani

Serves 4–6
360–240 calories per serving

20 ml (4 tsp) polyunsaturated oil

seeds of 4 cardamoms

5 ml (1 level tsp) cumin seeds

4 cloves

2.5 cm (1 inch) cinnamon stick

225 g (8 oz) brown or white basmati rice

450 ml (¾ pint) boiling vegetable stock

Don't let the length of this list of spices put you off—any large supermarket, delicatessen or ethnic shop should stock them.

1 Put half the oil, the cardamom seeds, cumin, cloves and cinnamon stick in a medium bowl. Microwave on HIGH for 30 seconds. Add the rice and coat in the fried spice mixture. Add the stock. Cover, leaving a gap to let steam escape, and microwave on HIGH for 30–35 minutes if using brown rice and 10–12 minutes if using white, or until tender, stirring once and adding a little extra water if necessary. Leave to stand, covered, while cooking the spices and vegetables.

2 garlic cloves, skinned

2.5 cm (1 inch) piece of fresh root ginger, peeled

1 medium onion, skinned and chopped

2.5 ml ($\frac{1}{2}$ level tsp) chilli powder

5 ml (1 level tsp) coriander seeds

2.5 ml ($\frac{1}{2}$ level tsp) ground turmeric

15 ml (1 level tbsp) poppy seeds

2 medium potatoes, scrubbed and cubed

175 g (6 oz) cauliflower florets

2 medium carrots, scrubbed and cubed

1 large green pepper, seeded and sliced

50 g (2 oz) French beans, cut into 2.5 cm (1 inch) pieces

2 large tomatoes, roughly chopped

100 g (4 oz) fresh or frozen peas

100 g (4 oz) button mushrooms, halved

150 ml ($\frac{1}{4}$ pint) low-fat natural yogurt

30 ml (2 tbsp) chopped fresh coriander

2 green chillies, seeded and finely chopped

60 ml (4 tbsp) lemon or lime juice

onion rings and fresh coriander, to garnish

2 Put the garlic, ginger, onion, chilli powder, coriander seeds, turmeric and poppy seeds in a blender or food processor with about 15 ml (1 tbsp) water and blend until smooth.

3 Put the remaining oil and the spice paste in a large ovenproof serving dish. Microwave on HIGH for 2 minutes, stirring frequently. Add the potatoes, cauliflower, carrots, green pepper and French beans. Cover, leaving a gap to let steam escape, and microwave on HIGH for 5 minutes. Add the tomatoes, peas and mushrooms and microwave on HIGH for 2 minutes. Gradually add the yogurt and chopped coriander.

4 Spoon the rice evenly over the vegetable mixture. Sprinkle with the chillies and pour over the lemon juice. DO NOT STIR. Re-cover and microwave on HIGH for 12–15 minutes until the vegetables are tender. Fluff up the rice with a fork and garnish with onion rings and coriander. Serve immediately.

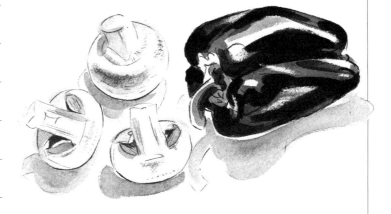

Grated Vegetable Terrine

Serves 4–6
290–193 calories per serving

350 g (12 oz) carrots, grated

350 g (12 oz) courgettes, grated

350 g (12 oz) leeks, very thinly sliced and washed

1 garlic clove, skinned and crushed

100 g (4 oz) fresh wholemeal breadcrumbs

100 g (4 oz) Cheddar cheese, grated

2 eggs, beaten

45 ml (3 tbsp) low-fat natural yogurt

30 ml (2 tbsp) chopped parsley

salt and pepper

This mixed vegetable terrine is very easy to make and cooks beautifully in the microwave, with the vegetables retaining all of their colour and flavour. It is equally good served as a cold starter for a summer meal.

1 Put the carrots, courgettes, leeks and garlic in a medium bowl with 15 ml (1 tbsp) water. Cover, leaving a gap to let steam escape, and microwave on HIGH for 7–9 minutes or until softened, stirring once.

2 Stir in the remaining ingredients and season with salt and pepper to taste. Beat thoroughly together.

3 Turn the mixture into a 900 g (2 lb) loaf dish and level the surface. Cover loosely with absorbent kitchen paper and microwave on HIGH for 8–10 minutes or until the surface feels firm. Leave to stand for 5 minutes, then turn out on to a serving plate to serve.

Individual Leek Tarts

Serves 4
243 calories per serving

75 g (3 oz) plain wholemeal flour

2.5 ml ($\frac{1}{2}$ level tsp) mustard powder

2.5 ml ($\frac{1}{2}$ level tsp) cayenne pepper (optional)

salt and pepper

40 g (1$\frac{1}{2}$ oz) polyunsaturated margarine

15 ml (1 level tbsp) medium oatmeal

350 g (12 oz) leeks, very thinly sliced and washed

1 egg

283 g (10 oz) silken tofu

Pastry is not usually successful in the microwave but this rather unconventional method works very well. The tarts are fragile, so handle with care.

1 To make the pastry, mix the flour, mustard, cayenne and salt and pepper to taste in a bowl. Rub in the margarine until the mixture resembles fine breadcrumbs. Stir in the oatmeal.

2 Stir in 30–45 ml (2–3 tbsp) water and mix together using a round bladed knife. Knead lightly to give a firm, smooth dough.

3 Roll out the dough very thinly on a lightly floured surface. Invert four 10 cm (4 inch) shallow glass flan dishes and use the dough to cover the base and sides of each. Cover and chill while making the filling.

4 To make the filling, put the leeks and 15 ml (1 tbsp) water in a medium bowl. Cover, leaving a gap to let steam escape, and microwave on HIGH for 10 minutes or until the leeks are very soft.

15 ml (1 tbsp) snipped chives

freshly grated nutmeg

snipped fresh chives, to garnish

5 Stir in the egg, tofu, chives and salt, pepper and nutmeg to taste. Beat well together and set aside.

6 Uncover the pastry cases and prick all over with a fork. Microwave on HIGH, pastry side uppermost, for 3–3½ minutes or until the pastry is firm to the touch. Leave to stand for 3 minutes. Carefully invert the pastry cases, removing the flan dishes, and fill with the leek and tofu mixture.

7 Arrange the tarts in a circle on the turntable or the base of the cooker. Microwave on HIGH for 5 minutes until firm.

8 Sprinkle with a little extra grated nutmeg and chives to garnish. Serve immediately with a tomato salad.

Pasta Verdi with Shredded Courgettes

Serves 2
507 calories per serving

225 g (8 oz) small dried green pasta shapes

salt and pepper

2 leeks, thinly sliced and washed

15 ml (1 tbsp) olive oil

225 g (8 oz) small courgettes

finely grated rind and juice of 1 lime

30 ml (2 tbsp) chopped fresh mixed herbs

25 g (1 oz) pine nuts (optional)

75 g (3 oz) Cheddar cheese, grated

Lime gives this dish a refreshingly, tangy flavour. It may also be served cold, without the cheese, as an accompaniment. If you are counting calories, omit the pine nuts to make this only 417 calories per serving.

1 Put the pasta and salt to taste in a large bowl, then pour over 1.1 litres (2 pints) boiling water. Microwave on HIGH for 8–10 minutes until almost tender. Leave to stand while making the sauce.

2 Put the leeks and oil in a large ovenproof serving bowl. Microwave on HIGH for 2–3 minutes until slightly softened.

3 Meanwhile, cut the courgettes into 4 cm (1½ inch) lengths, cut each length in half and then into very thin strips. Add to the leeks with the lime rind and juice, the herbs and pine nuts, if using. Season with salt and pepper to taste and microwave on HIGH for 1 minute, stirring once.

4 Drain the pasta and stir into the courgette mixture. Combine gently together and microwave on HIGH for 1–2 minutes until heated through. Spoon on to two warmed serving plates, sprinkle with the grated cheese and serve immediately.

Tofu and Bean Burgers

Makes 6
95 calories each

283 g (10 oz) silken tofu

397 g (14 oz) can red kidney beans, drained and rinsed

2.5 ml ($\frac{1}{2}$ tsp) miso

2.5 ml ($\frac{1}{2}$ tsp) yeast extract

5 ml (1 level tsp) dried mixed herbs

1 medium onion, skinned and grated

2 courgettes, grated

25 g (1 oz) wholemeal breadcrumbs

few drops of chilli sauce

1 egg, beaten

15 ml (1 tbsp) lemon juice

grated rind of 1 small lemon

pepper

Tofu, or soya bean curd, is a first–class source of protein. It is relatively low in carbohydrate and fat content, and contains calcium, iron and the B vitamins. This strange sounding combination makes very tasty burgers.

1 Put the tofu and kidney beans in a bowl and mash together using a potato masher or a fork. Dissolve the miso and yeast extract in 30 ml (2 tbsp) hot water and stir in with the remaining ingredients. Beat well together.

2 Shape the mixture into six burgers, about 2 cm ($\frac{3}{4}$ inch) thick.

3 Arrange the burgers in a circle around the edge of a large flat ovenproof plate. Microwave on HIGH for 8 minutes. Carefully turn them over and microwave on HIGH for a further 8 minutes. Serve hot with salad or in wholemeal rolls.

Gado-Gado

Serves 6
288 calories per serving

75 g (3 oz) natural peanut butter

50 g (2 oz) unsalted peanuts, chopped

15 ml (1 tbsp) shoyu sauce

juice of 1 lemon

1 garlic clove, skinned and crushed

5 ml (1 level tsp) ground cumin

5 ml (1 level tsp) chilli powder

50 g (2 oz) unsweetened desiccated coconut

225 g (8 oz) new potatoes, scrubbed

Gado-Gado is an Indonesian mixed salad served with a spicy peanut sauce. The vegetables used may be varied according to availability and personal preference, using both cooked vegetables and fresh salad ingredients. For a vegan meal, substitute the eggs with cubes of tofu.

1 To make the sauce, put the peanut butter, peanuts, shoyu sauce, lemon juice, garlic, cumin, chilli, coconut and 300 ml ($\frac{1}{2}$ pint) boiling water in a medium ovenproof serving bowl. Set aside.

2 Cut the potatoes into 0.5 cm ($\frac{1}{4}$ inch) slices and arrange around the edge of a shallow dish. Pour over 15 ml (1 tbsp) water. Cover, leaving a gap to let steam escape, and microwave on HIGH for 5 minutes or until almost tender.

3 Cut the carrots diagonally into 0.5 cm ($\frac{1}{4}$ inch) slices. Arrange the cauliflower, French beans and

225 g (8 oz) small carrots, scrubbed

100 g (4 oz) cauliflower florets

100 g (4 oz) French beans, trimmed and halved

½ crisp lettuce, shredded

50 g (2 oz) beansprouts

½ cucumber, cut into chunks

2 eggs, hard-boiled and quartered

carrots in the centre of the dish and add 30 ml (2 tbsp) water. Re-cover and microwave on HIGH for 7–9 minutes or until the vegetables are slightly softened.

4 Microwave the sauce on HIGH for 3–4 minutes until boiling and slightly thickened.

5 Meanwhile, arrange the lettuce on a plate and arrange the carrots, potatoes, cauliflower, beans, beansprouts, cucumber and eggs on top. Serve immediately with the sauce handed separately.

Pine Nut and Sage Stuffed Onions

Serves 4
296 calories per serving

8 medium onions, skinned

300 ml (½ pint) boiling vegetable stock

50 g (2 oz) pine nuts, finely chopped

75 g (3 oz) wholemeal breadcrumbs

15 ml (1 tbsp) chopped fresh sage or 5 ml (1 level tsp) dried

150 ml (¼ pint) low-fat natural yogurt

100 g (4 oz) Edam cheese, grated

salt and pepper

cayenne pepper

5 ml (1 level tsp) Dijon mustard

Pine nuts are the small, pale cream-coloured seeds of the Mediterranean pine tree. They have a distinctive flavour and a soft, oily texture quite unlike that of any other nut.

1 Put the onions and stock into a large shallow dish. Cover, leaving a gap to let steam escape, and microwave on HIGH for 15 minutes until tender. Remove the onions from the stock, using a slotted spoon, and cool slightly. Reserve the stock.

2 When the onions are cool enough to handle, carefully scoop out the centres, leaving a shell about 0.5 cm (¼ inch) thick.

3 Roughly chop the scooped-out onion and mix with the nuts, 50 g (2 oz) of the breadcrumbs, half of the sage, half of the yogurt and 25 g (1 oz) of the cheese. Season with salt, pepper and cayenne pepper.

4 Fill the onion shells with the mixture piling it up on top, if necessary. Return them to the dish with half of the stock. Cover, leaving a gap to let steam escape, and microwave on HIGH for 6–8 minutes, until completely heated through.

5 Mix the remaining cheese and breadcrumbs together and sprinkle over the onions. Transfer to a flameproof serving dish and brown under a hot grill.

6 Stir the remaining stock, sage, yogurt and the mustard into the liquid in the cooking dish. Microwave on HIGH for 1 minute until thickened. Season with salt and pepper to taste and serve with the onions.

Pasta with Walnut and Sage Sauce

Serves 4
424 calories per serving

400 g (14 oz) dried wholemeal pasta shapes

salt and pepper

10 ml (2 tsp) olive oil

150 g (5 oz) low-fat soft cheese

15 ml (1 tbsp) chopped fresh sage

50 g (2 oz) walnuts, finely chopped

sage sprigs, to garnish

All pasta is made from a special hard, high-protein wheat called durum wheat. Wholemeal pasta is made from the whole part of the wheat grains, and retains more of the natural nutrients than refined varieties.

1 Put the pasta and salt to taste in a large bowl. Pour over about 1.7 litres (3 pints) boiling water and stir. Cover, leaving a gap to let steam escape, and microwave on HIGH for 8–10 minutes or until just tender, stirring occasionally. Leave to stand, covered, while making the sauce. Do not drain.

2 To make the sauce, put the oil in a large ovenproof serving bowl. Microwave on HIGH for 30 seconds until hot. Stir in the cheese and microwave on HIGH for 1–2 minutes or until melted, stirring once.

3 Add the sage, walnuts and pepper to taste, and mix well together.

4 Drain the pasta and stir into the sauce. Toss together until the pasta is coated with the sauce. Microwave on HIGH for 1–2 minutes to heat through and serve immediately, garnished with sage sprigs. Accompany with a green salad.

Broccoli Timbale

Serves 4
157 calories per serving

450 g (1 lb) broccoli

1 medium onion, skinned and roughly chopped

1 garlic clove, skinned and crushed

75 g (3 oz) low-fat soft cheese

3 eggs

50 g (2 oz) fresh wholemeal breadcrumbs

pinch of freshly grated nutmeg

salt and pepper

A timbale is generally used to describe a dish which is baked and then turned out of its cooking dish—in this recipe a ring mould is used for attractive presentation.

1 Thinly slice the broccoli stalks and divide the heads into small florets.

2 Put the broccoli, onion, garlic and 300 ml ($\frac{1}{2}$ pint) water in a large bowl. Cover, leaving a gap to let steam escape, and microwave on HIGH for 12 minutes until tender. Allow to cool slightly.

3 Put the broccoli and liquid in a blender or food processor and work until smooth. Add the cheese, eggs, breadcrumbs, nutmeg and salt and pepper to taste and mix together.

4 Spoon the mixture into a 1.1 litre (2 pint) ring mould and microwave on HIGH for 13–15 minutes or until set.

5 Leave to stand for 5 minutes, then turn out on to a warmed serving plate. Serve sliced with wholemeal bread and a tomato salad.

Spiced Lentils with Cauliflower

Serves 4
175 calories per serving

15 ml (1 tbsp) polyunsaturated oil

5 ml (1 level tsp) cumin seeds, lightly crushed

2.5 ml ($\frac{1}{2}$ level tsp) ground turmeric

5 ml (1 level tsp) ground cardamom

15 ml (1 level tbsp) poppy seeds

100 g (4 oz) split red lentils

450 ml ($\frac{3}{4}$ pint) boiling vegetable stock

1 green chilli, seeded and chopped

1 garlic clove, skinned and crushed

1 small cauliflower, cut into small florets

100 g (4 oz) cottage cheese

100 g (4 oz) frozen peas

30 ml (2 tbsp) chopped fresh coriander

salt and pepper

sliced onion and fresh coriander, to garnish

Split lentils can be cooked very successfully in a microwave, unlike pulses totally enclosed in a skin which tend to burst and toughen when cooked. Serve this dish as part of a vegetarian meal: Chick peas with tomatoes (page 108) or Root vegetables with sesame seeds (page 74) would complement the flavours well.

1 Put the oil, cumin, turmeric, cardamom and poppy seeds in a large bowl. Microwave on HIGH for 1 minute, stirring once.

2 Add the lentils, stock, chilli and garlic. Cover, leaving a gap to let steam escape, and microwave on HIGH for 12–14 minutes or until the lentils are almost tender, stirring once.

3 Stir in the cauliflower, cottage cheese and peas. Re-cover and microwave on HIGH for 7–9 minutes or until the cauliflower is tender, stirring once. Stir in the chopped coriander and season with salt and pepper to taste. Garnish with onion slices and coriander and serve with brown rice.

Root Vegetables with Sesame Seeds

Serves 6
198 calories per serving

15 ml (1 tbsp) sunflower oil

5 ml (1 level tsp) paprika

60 ml (4 tbsp) sesame seeds

450 g (1 lb) medium onions, skinned

225 g (8 oz) carrots, scrubbed

225 g (8 oz) parsnips, peeled

225 g (8 oz) turnips, peeled

225 g (8 oz) swede, peeled

salt and pepper

100 g (4 oz) Cheddar cheese, grated

Sesame seeds are exceptionally high in protein, potassium and calcium. The proportions of vegetables in this dish may be varied, but be sure to keep the total weight the same.

1 Put the oil, paprika and sesame seeds in a small bowl. Microwave on HIGH for 2 minutes until the sesame seeds are lightly browned, stirring once.

2 Cut the onions into quarters, and the carrots and parsnips into 5 × 1 cm (2 × ½ inch) lengths. Cut the turnips and swede into 1 cm (½ inch) cubes.

3 Put all of the vegetables into a large ovenproof serving bowl with 30 ml (2 tbsp) water. Cover, leaving a gap to let steam escape, and microwave on HIGH for 18–20 minutes or until tender, stirring occasionally.

4 Season with salt and pepper to taste, pour over the sesame seed and oil mixture and toss together until all the vegetables are coated. Sprinkle with the grated cheese and serve hot.

Bean Goulash

Serves 4–6
246–164 calories per serving

100 g (4 oz) black-eye beans, soaked overnight

100 g (4 oz) aduki beans, soaked overnight

15 ml (1 tbsp) sunflower oil

1 garlic clove, skinned and crushed

1 yellow pepper, seeded and roughly chopped

10 ml (2 level tsp) caraway seeds, lightly crushed

15 ml (1 level tbsp) paprika

397 g (14 oz) can chopped tomatoes

175 g (6 oz) mushrooms, thickly sliced

To save time, you can substitute both kinds of beans for the canned varieties. Use three 397 g (14 oz) cans of your choice and proceed from step 2.

1 Drain the beans and put into a large bowl. Pour over enough boiling water to cover and come about 2.5 cm (1 inch) above the beans. Cover, leaving a gap to let steam escape, and microwave on HIGH for 25–30 minutes until tender. Leave to stand, covered. Do not drain.

2 Meanwhile, put the oil, garlic, yellow pepper, caraway seeds and paprika in a large ovenproof serving bowl. Cover, leaving a gap to let steam escape, and microwave on HIGH for 2 minutes, stirring once.

3 Drain the beans, rinse with boiling water and add to the pepper with the tomatoes and mushrooms. Re-cover and microwave on HIGH for 8–10 minutes, stirring once. Stir in 30 ml (2 tbsp) of the yogurt and season with salt and pepper to taste.

60 ml (4 tbsp) low-fat natural yogurt

salt and pepper

chopped fresh parsley, to garnish

Drizzle the remaining yogurt on top and sprinkle with the parsley. Serve hot with brown rice.

Burghul with Mange-Tout and Mushrooms

Serves 4
324 calories per serving

15 ml (1 tbsp) polyunsaturated oil

1 medium onion, skinned and finely chopped

1 garlic clove, skinned and crushed

225 g (8 oz) burghul wheat

1 eating apple, coarsely grated

2 large carrots, scrubbed and coarsely grated

100 g (4 oz) flat mushrooms, coarsely chopped

100 g (4 oz) mange-tout, topped, tailed and halved

30 ml (2 tbsp) chopped fresh coriander

75 ml (5 tbsp) low-fat natural yogurt

25 g (1 oz) chopped mixed nuts

salt and pepper

50 g (2 oz) Edam cheese, coarsely grated

chopped fresh coriander, to garnish

Burghul wheat is also known as bulghur or bulgar wheat. It is made from whole wheat grains that have been soaked and then baked until they crack into small particles.

1 Put the oil, onion and garlic in a large bowl. Cover, leaving a gap to let steam escape, and microwave on HIGH for 5–7 minutes until softened.

2 Stir in the burghul wheat, apple, carrot, mushrooms and 150 ml ($\frac{1}{4}$ pint) boiling water. Re-cover and microwave on HIGH for 14–15 minutes until softened, stirring occasionally.

3 Stir in the mange-tout and microwave on HIGH for 1–2 minutes or until just tender.

4 Beat the coriander and yogurt together. Stir into the burghul wheat mixture with the nuts and salt and pepper to taste. Mix well together and sprinkle with the cheese. Serve hot, garnished with coriander. Accompany with a green salad.

Marinated Vegetable and Tofu Kebabs

Serves 4
160 calories per serving

225 g (8 oz) firm tofu

8 small courgettes, trimmed

12 fresh or canned baby
sweetcorns

16 button mushrooms

12 cherry tomatoes

8 bay leaves

30 ml (2 tbsp) tahini paste

20 ml (4 tsp) shoyu or soya
sauce

20 ml (4 tsp) cider vinegar

1 garlic clove, skinned and
crushed

1 cm (½ inch) fresh root ginger,
crushed

10 ml (2 tsp) clear honey

Tofu is made from soya beans and is used extensively in oriental cooking for its nutritive value. Be sure to use firm, not silken, tofu for this recipe. Weight for weight, tofu contains as much protein as meat, yet it is very low in fat.

1 Cut the tofu into 16 cubes. Cut each courgette into four pieces.

2 Thread the vegetables, tofu and bay leaves on to eight wooden skewers, alternating the ingredients as much as possible.

3 Whisk all the remaining ingredients together and pour into a large shallow dish.

4 Arrange the kebabs in the dish in a single layer and turn to coat in the marinade. Leave to marinate for 1–2 hours, turning occasionally.

5 Cover with a double thickness of absorbent kitchen paper. Microwave on HIGH for 7 minutes until the vegetables are tender, turning 2–3 times during cooking. Serve the kebabs, with the marinade spooned over, on a bed of brown rice.

Wholemeal Pasta with Cheese and Cashew Nuts

Serves 2–3
612–408 calories per serving

225 g (8 oz) fresh wholemeal
tagliatelle

salt and pepper

15 ml (1 tbsp) polyunsaturated
oil

50 g (2 oz) cashew nuts

1 medium onion, skinned and
finely chopped

1 garlic clove, skinned and
finely chopped

225 g (8 oz) fromage frais

Time is not saved by cooking pasta in a microwave cooker, nevertheless it does mean there is no risk of sticking or of the water boiling over, and the results are excellent.

1 Put the tagliatelle in a large bowl. Pour over about 1.7 litres (3 pints) boiling water and add salt to taste. Cover, leaving a gap to let steam escape, and microwave on HIGH for 3–4 minutes until just tender. Leave to stand, covered. Do not drain.

2 Meanwhile, put the oil, nuts, onion and garlic in a medium bowl. Cover, leaving a gap to let steam escape, and microwave on HIGH for 5–6 minutes until the onion has softened and the nuts are lightly browned, stirring frequently.

60 ml (4 tbsp) chopped fresh basil or parsley

15 ml (1 level tbsp) grated fresh Parmesan cheese

chopped fresh basil or parsley, to garnish

3 Drain the pasta and return to the bowl. Add the nut mixture, cheese and herbs and season with pepper to taste. Toss together then microwave on HIGH for 1–2 minutes to heat through. Serve immediately, sprinkled with the Parmesan cheese and chopped herbs to garnish. Accompany with a green salad.

Lentil, Aubergine and Potato Pie

Serves 4
298 calories per serving

3 medium potatoes, each weighing about 225 g (8 oz), scrubbed

100 g (4 oz) split red lentils

1 medium onion, skinned and finely chopped

1 bay leaf

5 ml (1 level tsp) dried thyme

15 ml (1 level tbsp) tomato purée

1 small aubergine, coarsely chopped

450 ml (¾ pint) boiling vegetable stock

100 g (4 oz) French beans, trimmed and cut into 2.5 cm (1 inch) lengths

60 ml (4 tbsp) skimmed milk

salt and pepper

25 g (1 oz) grated fresh Parmesan cheese

This substantial, hearty dish is a vegetarian version of shepherd's pie. Don't throw away the potato skins in step 3, but cut them into neat strips and grill for 2–3 minutes on each side until crisp. Eat as a snack or serve with a dip.

1 Prick the potatoes all over with a fork and arrange in a circle on a sheet of absorbent kitchen paper. Microwave on HIGH for 10–15 minutes or until soft, turning over halfway through cooking. Set aside to cool slightly.

2 While the potatoes are cooling, put the lentils, onion, bay leaf, thyme, tomato purée, aubergine and vegetable stock in a large bowl and mix well together. Cover, leaving a gap to let steam escape, and microwave on HIGH for 20–25 minutes or until the lentils and aubergine are tender and most of the liquid is absorbed. Add the beans and microwave on HIGH for 2 minutes.

3 Meanwhile, cut the potatoes in half and scoop out the flesh into a bowl. Mash with the milk and season with salt and pepper to taste.

4 Spoon the lentil and aubergine mixture into a flameproof serving dish. Spoon over the mashed potato and sprinkle with the cheese. Microwave on HIGH for 1–2 minutes or until heated through then brown under a hot grill if wished. Serve hot with a green vegetable.

Spaghetti with Tomato Sauce

Serves 2–3
453–302 calories per serving

1 medium onion, skinned and finely chopped

1 celery stick, trimmed and finely chopped

1 medium carrot, scrubbed and finely chopped

1 garlic clove, skinned and crushed

227 g (8 oz) can tomatoes

150 ml ($\frac{1}{4}$ pint) boiling vegetable stock

15 ml (1 level tbsp) tomato purée

2.5 ml ($\frac{1}{2}$ level tsp) dried oregano

salt and pepper

225 g (8 oz) dried wholemeal spaghetti

30 ml (2 level tbsp) grated fresh Parmesan cheese

The flavour of this classic tomato sauce is improved if it is made in advance and reheated just before serving.

1 Put the onion, celery, carrot, garlic, tomatoes with their juice, stock, tomato purée, oregano and salt and pepper to taste in a medium bowl. Cover, leaving a gap to let steam escape, and microwave on HIGH for 15–20 minutes until the vegetables have softened, stirring occasionally. Leave to cool slightly while cooking the spaghetti.

2 Put the spaghetti in a large bowl and pour over about 1.1 litres (2 pints) boiling water and add salt to taste. Stir, bending the spaghetti around the bowl so that it is all covered with water. Cover, leaving a gap to let steam escape, then microwave on HIGH for 7–8 minutes until just tender. Leave to stand, covered, for 5 minutes. Do not drain.

3 While the spaghetti is standing, put the sauce in a blender or food processor and work until smooth. Pour back into the bowl and microwave on HIGH for 2 minutes until hot.

4 Drain the spaghetti and turn into a warmed serving dish. Pour over the sauce, sprinkle with the Parmesan cheese and serve immediately with a salad.

Transparent Noodles with Vegetables and Tofu

Serves 4
120 calories per serving

15 ml (1 tbsp) shoyu sauce

1–2 garlic cloves, skinned and crushed

30 ml (2 tbsp) dry sherry

450 ml ($\frac{3}{4}$ pint) vegetable stock

225 g (8 oz) firm tofu, cut into 2.5 cm (1 inch) cubes

3 large carrots, scrubbed and thinly sliced

Transparent or cellophane noodles are made from mung-bean starch paste. Mooli is a long white radish-like vegetable. Both of these rather unusual ingredients can be bought from oriental food shops.

1 Put the shoyu, garlic, sherry and 150 ml ($\frac{1}{4}$ pint) of the stock in a large bowl. Stir in the tofu and mix well together. Leave to marinate for 3–4 hours or overnight.

2 Remove the tofu from the marinade with a slotted spoon and set aside. Add the vegetables to the marinade and mix well together.

3 Cover, leaving a gap to let steam escape, and microwave on HIGH for 5 minutes or until soft.

225 g (8 oz) green cabbage,
finely shredded

100 g (4 oz) mooli, scrubbed
and thinly sliced

50 g (2 oz) transparent noodles

4 Stir in the noodles, remaining stock and the tofu. Microwave on HIGH for 7–10 minutes until the noodles are softened. Serve immediately.

Vegetable Chilli

Serves 4–6
97–64 calories per serving

1 green chilli, seeded and
chopped

1 medium onion, skinned and
thinly sliced

1 garlic clove, skinned and
crushed

3 celery sticks, trimmed and
sliced

4 ripe tomatoes, roughly
chopped

10 ml (2 level tsp) tomato
purée

2.5–5 ml ($\frac{1}{2}$–1 level tsp) chilli
powder

5 cm (2 inch) cinnamon stick

5 ml (1 level tsp) ground cumin

5 ml (1 level tsp) dried oregano

150 ml ($\frac{1}{4}$ pint) boiling
vegetable stock

1 green pepper, seeded and
chopped

100 g (4 oz) button mushrooms

225 g (8 oz) cauliflower florets

3 courgettes, sliced

225 g (8 oz) cooked red kidney
beans or 425 g (15 oz) can red
kidney beans, drained and
rinsed

30 ml (2 tbsp) chopped fresh
coriander (optional)

salt and pepper

A vegetarian version of the famous Mexican dish. Use a selection of vegetables in season or vary according to personal taste. The vegetables used here provide a good contrast of colours and textures.

1 Put the chilli, onion, garlic, celery, tomatoes, tomato purée, chilli powder, cinnamon stick, cumin, oregano and stock in a large ovenproof serving dish. Mix well together. Cover, leaving a gap to let steam escape, and microwave on HIGH for 8–10 minutes or until the tomatoes are very mushy, stirring occasionally.

2 Stir in the remaining ingredients and season with salt and pepper to taste. Re-cover and microwave on HIGH for 15–20 minutes or until the vegetables are tender, stirring occasionally. Serve hot with brown rice.

Spinach and Black-Eye Bean Stew

Serves 4–6
258–172 calories per serving

225 g (8 oz) black-eye beans, soaked overnight

15 ml (1 tbsp) polyunsaturated oil

2 medium onions, skinned and cut into eighths

1 small garlic clove, skinned and crushed

450 g (1 lb) spinach, washed, trimmed and shredded, or 225 g (8 oz) frozen spinach, thawed

60 ml (4 tbsp) low-fat natural yogurt

75 g (3 oz) Cheddar cheese, grated

freshly grated nutmeg

ground allspice

salt and pepper

Pulses are an important source of protein in a vegetarian diet. Combined with a grain product, such as brown rice, this dish will provide protein that is just as good as a meat or fish meal. Remember to wash spinach well as it collects dirt. Use several changes of water and handle the leaves gently as they bruise easily.

1 Drain the beans and put into a large bowl. Pour over enough boiling water to cover and come about 2.5 cm (1 inch) above the level of the beans. Cover, leaving a gap to let steam escape, and microwave on HIGH for 25–30 minutes or until tender, stirring once. Leave to stand, covered. Do not drain.

2 While the beans are standing, put the oil, onion and garlic in a large ovenproof serving bowl. Microwave on HIGH for 5 minutes until the onion is slightly softened, stirring once.

3 Drain the beans, rinse with boiling water and stir into the onion. Mix well together. Cover, leaving a gap to let steam escape, and microwave on HIGH for 8–10 minutes or until the onion is soft.

4 Stir in the spinach and microwave, uncovered, on HIGH for 2 minutes or until the spinach is just cooked. Stir in the yogurt and cheese and season generously with nutmeg and allspice and salt and pepper to taste. Serve hot with brown rice.

Mexican Baked Potatoes

Serves 4
335 calories per serving

1 medium onion, skinned and finely chopped

1 garlic clove, skinned and crushed

397 g (14 oz) can tomatoes

10 ml (2 level tsp) tomato purée

1 green chilli, seeded and chopped

2.5 ml ($\frac{1}{2}$ level tsp) ground cumin

The rich tomato and bean sauce turns this into a hearty, sustaining meal. If you cannot find fresh chillies, use 2.5 ml ($\frac{1}{2}$ level tsp) chilli powder.

1 Put the onion, garlic, tomatoes, tomato purée, chilli and cumin in a large bowl. Mix thoroughly together. Microwave on HIGH for 10–12 minutes until reduced and thickened. Stir in the beans and cook for a further 2 minutes. Season with salt and pepper to taste. Leave to stand while cooking the potatoes.

2 Prick the potatoes all over with a fork and place on absorbent kitchen paper. Microwave on HIGH for 10–15 minutes or until soft, turning over halfway through cooking.

100 g (4 oz) cooked red kidney beans or 432 g (15 oz) can red kidney beans, drained and rinsed

salt and pepper

4 medium potatoes, each weighing about 175 g (6 oz), scrubbed

1 small ripe avocado (optional)

50 g (2 oz) Edam cheese, grated

3 Cut the potatoes in half lengthways. Place on four ovenproof serving plates and divide the chilli bean mixture between them, letting it spill out on to the plates.

4 Microwave two plates at a time on HIGH for 1–2 minutes until heated through.

5 Halve, stone and peel the avocado, and slice the flesh. Arrange a few slices on top of each potato, then sprinkle with the cheese. Serve the potatoes hot with a mixed salad.

Pasta with Spinach and Ricotta

Serves 2

546 calories per serving

450 g (1 lb) fresh spinach, washed, or 225 g (8 oz) frozen leaf spinach

225 g (8 oz) fresh green tagliatelle

salt and pepper

15 ml (1 tbsp) olive oil

1 garlic clove, skinned and crushed

1 small onion, skinned and finely chopped

100 g (4 oz) ricotta cheese

5 ml (1 tsp) chopped fresh marjoram (optional)

freshly grated nutmeg

Both spinach and ricotta cheese are used extensively in Italian cooking and are often cooked with pasta. Low-fat ricotta is made from the whey left over from cheese production.

1 If using fresh spinach, shred the leaves into small pieces. Set aside.

2 Put the tagliatelle in a large bowl. Pour over about 1.7 litres (3 pints) boiling water, add salt to taste and stir. Cover, leaving a gap to let steam escape, and microwave on HIGH for 3–4 minutes until just tender. Leave to stand, covered. Do not drain.

3 Meanwhile, put the oil, garlic and onion in a medium bowl. Cover, leaving a gap to let steam escape, and microwave on HIGH for 4–5 minutes or until softened, stirring occasionally.

4 Stir in the spinach and microwave on HIGH for a further 5 minutes if using fresh spinach and 7–8 minutes if using frozen, stirring occasionally. Set aside.

5 Drain the pasta and return to the bowl. Crumble in the ricotta cheese. Add the spinach mixture, marjoram if using and nutmeg and pepper to taste. Toss together then microwave on HIGH for 1–2 minutes to heat through. Serve immediately with a green salad.

Feta Cheese and Brown Rice Ring

Serves 4–6
383–255 calories per serving

225 g (8 oz) long-grain brown rice

salt and pepper

15 ml (1 tbsp) olive oil

30 ml (2 level tbsp) mild wholegrain mustard

juice of 1 lemon

2 celery sticks, trimmed and finely sliced

100 g (4 oz) feta cheese, crumbled

25 g (1 oz) pumpkin seeds

25 g (1 oz) sunflower seeds

225 g (8 oz) small button mushrooms, finely sliced

30 ml (2 tbsp) chopped fresh mixed herbs, such as coriander, mint, parsley

Feta cheese was originally made from ewes' milk in Greece, but now it is made in several countries. It is stored in barrels in brine, so season sparingly with salt. Feta cheese is also lower in fat than most hard cheeses, about 55 calories per 25 g (1 oz) compared with an average of 100 calories per 25 g (1 oz) for hard cheeses like Cheddar and Gouda.

1 Put the rice and salt to taste in a large bowl. Pour over 450 ml ($\frac{3}{4}$ pint) boiling water and stir. Cover, leaving a gap to let steam escape, and microwave on HIGH for 30–35 minutes or until tender, stirring once and adding a little extra water if necessary. Leave to stand for 5 minutes by which time all the water should be absorbed.

2 Meanwhile, whisk the oil, mustard and lemon juice together.

3 Pour the dressing over the hot rice and mix together. Stir in the remaining ingredients and season with salt and pepper to taste. Toss together lightly with a fork.

4 Spoon the rice mixture into a lightly oiled 750 ml (1$\frac{1}{4}$ pint) ring mould, pressing it down firmly with the back of a spoon so that the ingredients cling together. Chill for at least 1 hour.

5 To serve, place a serving plate on top of the ring mould and invert so that the rice ring turns out on to the plate. Serve at room temperature with a colourful mixed salad.

CHAPTER 7

Meat and Poultry Main Courses

Lamb and Wheat Stew

Serves 4
355 calories per serving

225 g (8 oz) wholewheat grain, soaked for at least 8 hours or overnight

450 g (1 lb) lean lamb fillet

5 large tomatoes, roughly chopped

2 whole cloves

2.5 ml ($\frac{1}{2}$ level tsp) ground cinnamon

450 ml ($\frac{3}{4}$ pint) boiling lamb or chicken stock

salt and pepper

chopped fresh parsley, to garnish

This interesting stew makes a hearty main dish which needs only bread as an accompaniment to mop up the juices. End the meal with a fresh fruit salad to provide vitamin C and to refresh the palate.

1 Drain and rinse the wholewheat grain. Trim all excess fat from the meat and cut into 1 cm ($\frac{1}{2}$ inch) pieces.

2 Put the lamb and the remaining ingredients in a large bowl. Cover, leaving a gap to let steam escape, and microwave on HIGH for 20–25 minutes or until the lamb and wheat are very tender, stirring occasionally.

3 Using a slotted spoon, transfer the lamb and wheat to an ovenproof serving dish and set aside.

4 Microwave the cooking liquid on HIGH for 2–3 minutes until reduced and slightly thickened. Skim off any excess fat from the surface and discard.

5 Pour the reduced sauce over the lamb and wheat, then reheat on HIGH for 2 minutes. Garnish with the chopped parsley and serve hot with chunks of wholemeal bread.

Lamb with Aubergine and Mint

Serves 4
268 calories per serving

1 large aubergine, weighing about 400 g (14 oz)

salt and pepper

450 g (1 lb) lean boneless lamb, such as fillet or leg

30 ml (2 tbsp) olive oil

397 g (14 oz) can tomatoes, drained

few allspice berries, crushed

small bunch of fresh mint

It is essential to make this dish using fresh mint, dried does not have such a good flavour.

1 Cut the aubergine into 2.5 cm (1 inch) cubes. Put in a colander, sprinkling each layer generously with salt. Stand the colander on a large plate, cover with a small plate and place a weight on top. Leave for about 20 minutes to extract the bitter juices.

2 Meanwhile, trim the meat of all excess fat and cut into 2.5 cm (1 inch) cubes. Rinse the aubergine and pat dry.

3 Heat a large browning dish on HIGH for 5–8 minutes or according to manufacturer's instructions.

4 Put the oil in the browning dish, then quickly add the meat. Microwave on HIGH for 2 minutes.

5 Turn the pieces of meat over and microwave on HIGH for a further 2 minutes.

6 Add the aubergine to the browning dish and microwave on HIGH for 5 minutes, stirring once.

7 Add the tomatoes, breaking them up with a fork, the allspice and pepper to taste. Cover, leaving a gap to let steam escape, and microwave on HIGH for about 15 minutes or until the lamb and aubergine are very tender, stirring occasionally.

8 Coarsely chop the mint and stir into the lamb with salt to taste. Re-cover and microwave on HIGH for 1 minute. Serve hot with brown rice.

Garlic Studded Lamb with Mint

Serves 2
455 calories per serving

2 garlic cloves, skinned

1 rack of lamb, with 6 cutlets, chined and trimmed of excess fat

salt and pepper

15 ml (1 tbsp) polyunsaturated oil

75 ml (3 fl oz) chicken stock

5 ml (1 level tsp) Dijon mustard

15 ml (1 tbsp) chopped fresh mint

mint sprigs, to garnish

This is a delicious dish to make for a special dinner for two. Ask your butcher to chine and trim the meat. The garlic flavours the meat well as slivers of garlic are pressed into the fat of the lamb before cooking.

1 Cut the garlic cloves into slivers. Using the point of a sharp knife, pierce the fat on the lamb in about 12 places then insert the garlic slivers. Season well with pepper.

2 Heat a large browning dish on HIGH for 5–8 minutes or according to manufacturer's instructions.

3 Put the oil in the browning dish then quickly add the lamb, fat side down. Microwave on HIGH for 1 minute.

4 Turn the meat over and microwave on HIGH for 5–7 minutes or until just cooked. The meat should still be slightly pink in the centre. Transfer the meat to a warmed serving dish.

5 Add the chicken stock, mustard and mint to the dish and mix together, stirring, to loosen any sediment at the bottom of the dish. Season with salt and pepper to taste.

6 Microwave on HIGH for 1 minute until hot, stirring once. Slice the lamb into cutlets, spoon over the sauce and garnish with mint sprigs.

Bobotie

Serves 4
430 calories per serving

25 g (1 oz) flaked almonds

450 g (1 lb) lean minced beef

1 small onion, skinned and roughly chopped

2 thick slices of wholemeal bread, crusts removed

60 ml (4 tbsp) skimmed milk

2 large eating apples, peeled and chopped

50 g (2 oz) sultanas

5 ml (1 level tsp) poppy seeds

5 ml (1 level tsp) ground turmeric

5 ml (1 level tsp) fenugreek seeds

10 ml (2 level tsp) ground coriander

10 ml (2 level tsp) ground cumin

2.5 ml (½ level tsp) chilli powder (optional)

salt and pepper

1 egg

300 ml (½ pint) low-fat natural yogurt

Bobotie is a traditional South African dish. It can also be made using leftover lean cooked minced beef or lamb—simply omit the 5 minutes cooking time in step 2.

1 Put the flaked almonds on a large flat ovenproof plate. Microwave on HIGH for 6–8 minutes or until lightly browned, stirring occasionally. Set aside.

2 Put the beef and onion in a 2.3 litre (4 pint) ovenproof serving dish, about 20.5 cm (8 inches) in diameter. Microwave on HIGH for 7 minutes, stirring once. Drain off any excess fat and stir thoroughly to break up any large lumps of meat.

3 Soak the bread in the milk for 2–3 minutes, then squeeze with your fingers to remove most of the milk. Reserve the milk and add the bread to the meat with the apples, sultanas and spices.

4 Cover, leaving a gap to let steam escape, and microwave on HIGH for 10 minutes, stirring once. Season with salt and pepper to taste.

5 Mix the reserved milk with the egg and yogurt and pour over the mince mixture.

6 Sprinkle with the almonds and microwave on HIGH for 6–7 minutes or until the topping is set. Serve hot straight from the dish.

Lamb with Dates

Serves 4
304 calories per serving

15 g (½ oz) whole blanched almonds

100 g (4 oz) stoned dried dates, chopped

1.25 ml (¼ level tsp) ground cinnamon

finely grated rind and juice of 1 lime

A purée of dried dates makes a rich brown gravy without the use of stock cubes and browning agents. Unusual, but both tasty and nutritious, with the dates providing fibre, natural sweetness, vitamin A and some B vitamins.

1 Spread the almonds on a large ovenproof plate. Microwave on HIGH for 8–9 minutes or until browned, stirring occasionally.

2 Put the dates, cinnamon, lime rind and juice and 300 ml (½ pint) water in a small bowl. Cover, leaving

450 g (1 lb) lamb fillet

15 ml (1 tbsp) polyunsaturated oil

salt and pepper

lime wedges, to garnish

a gap to let steam escape, and microwave on HIGH for 4–5 minutes or until the dates are soft. Put the date and lime mixture into a blender or food processor and work until smooth.

3 Heat a large browning dish on HIGH for 5–8 minutes or according to manufacturer's instructions.

4 Meanwhile, trim the lamb of all excess fat and cut into 1 cm ($\frac{1}{2}$ inch) slices. Bat each slice out slightly using a rolling pin.

5 Put the oil and lamb into the browning dish. Microwave on HIGH for 2 minutes. Turn the meat over and microwave on HIGH for 2 minutes.

6 Add the date and lime mixture to the lamb. Season with salt and pepper to taste.

7 Cover, leaving a gap to let steam escape, and microwave on HIGH for 10 minutes or until the lamb is tender, stirring occasionally.

8 To serve, scatter the almonds over the lamb and garnish with the lime wedges.

Marinated Beef with Mange-tout and Walnuts

Serves 2
290 calories per serving

175 g (6 oz) lean sirloin

30 ml (2 tbsp) dry sherry

30 ml (2 tbsp) shoyu sauce

1 garlic clove, skinned and crushed

1 cm ($\frac{1}{2}$ inch) piece fresh root ginger, peeled and grated

100 g (4 oz) mange-tout, topped and tailed

25 g (1 oz) walnuts, roughly chopped

pepper

Marinating meat in this dish not only improves the texture and flavour but shortens the cooking time, too.

1 Trim the meat of all excess fat, then cut across the grain into very thin strips about 5 cm (2 inches) long. Put in a medium bowl with the sherry, shoyu sauce, garlic and ginger. Cover and leave to marinate for at least 1 hour.

2 Uncover the beef slightly, leaving a gap to let steam escape, and microwave on HIGH for 3 minutes, stirring once.

3 Add the remaining ingredients and microwave on HIGH for 3–4 minutes or until the beef is tender and the mange-tout just cooked, stirring once. Serve immediately with brown rice.

Sweet and Sour Pork

Serves 4
262 calories per serving

450 g (1 lb) pork fillet or tenderloin

15 ml (1 tbsp) polyunsaturated oil

2.5 cm (1 inch) piece fresh root ginger, finely chopped

1 garlic clove, skinned and crushed

1 small green pepper, seeded and cut into matchsticks

1 small red pepper, seeded and cut into matchsticks

3 spring onions, trimmed and cut into 2.5 cm (1 inch) lengths

227 g (8 oz) can water chestnuts, drained and quartered

10 ml (2 level tsp) cornflour

30 ml (2 tbsp) wine vinegar

15 ml (1 tbsp) clear honey

15 ml (1 level tbsp) tomato purée

30 ml (2 tbsp) orange or pineapple juice

15 ml (1 tbsp) shoyu sauce

This microwave adaptation of the traditionally deep-fried recipe produces a lighter, fresher dish, while still retaining the authentic flavour.

1 Heat a large browning dish on HIGH for 5–8 minutes or according to manufacturer's instructions.

2 Trim all fat and gristle from the pork and cut the meat across the grain into very thin strips, about 4 cm ($1\frac{1}{2}$ inches) long and 0.5 cm ($\frac{1}{4}$ inch) wide.

3 Add the oil to the browning dish then the meat, ginger and garlic and stir well. Microwave on HIGH for 3 minutes until just cooked, stirring once.

4 Stir in the peppers, spring onions and water chestnuts and microwave on HIGH for 3 minutes.

5 Mix the remaining ingredients together with 30 ml (2 tbsp) water and stir into the pork and vegetables. Microwave on HIGH for 3 minutes or until the sauce thickens, stirring twice. Serve at once with brown rice.

Pork and Sauerkraut Goulash

Serves 6
240 calories per serving

450 g (1 lb) pork fillet or tenderloin

15 ml (1 tbsp) polyunsaturated oil

150 ml ($\frac{1}{4}$ pint) boiling chicken stock

150 ml ($\frac{1}{4}$ pint) dry white wine

Pork fillet is a very tender, lean cut. It cooks quickly and is therefore ideal for cooking in a microwave. You may also see it sold as pork tenderloin.

1 Trim the meat of all excess fat and cut into 1 cm ($\frac{1}{2}$ inch) slices. Bat out slightly using a rolling pin.

2 Heat a large browning dish on HIGH for 5–8 minutes or according to manufacturer's instructions.

30 ml (2 level tbsp) paprika

5 ml (1 level tsp) caraway seeds

2 red eating apples, cored and sliced

45 ml (3 level tbsp) tomato purée

salt and pepper

2 medium onions, skinned and thinly sliced

936 g (2 lb) bottled or canned sauerkraut, drained and rinsed

150 ml ($\frac{1}{4}$ pint) Greek strained yogurt

3 Put the oil and pork in the browning dish. Microwave on HIGH for 2 minutes. Turn the pork over and microwave on HIGH for 2 minutes.

4 Add the remaining ingredients, except for the sauerkraut and yogurt and stir thoroughly, loosening any sediment at the bottom of the dish. Cover, leaving a gap to let steam escape, and microwave on HIGH for 13–15 minutes until the pork is tender, stirring occasionally.

5 Stir in the sauerkraut, cover, leaving a gap to let steam escape, and microwave on HIGH for 5 minutes, stirring occasionally.

6 Transfer to a warmed serving dish and serve immediately with the yogurt.

Liver with Satsumas

Serves 4
250 calories per serving

2 satsumas or tangerines

450 g (1 lb) lamb's or calf's liver, sliced

pepper

30 ml (2 tbsp) polyunsaturated oil

1 medium onion, skinned and sliced

30 ml (2 tbsp) chopped fresh parsley

Liver contains the mineral iron. When eaten with food containing vitamin C, as in the satsumas of this recipe, the absorption of iron is enhanced.

1 Using a sharp knife, pare the rind from the satsumas then cut into thin strips. Alternatively, use a lemon zester.

2 Peel and divide the satsumas into segments. If using tangerines, remove the pips.

3 Cut the liver lengthways into pencil-thin strips, trimming away all ducts and gristle. Season with pepper to taste.

4 Put the oil in a shallow dish and microwave on HIGH for 30 seconds. Stir in the onion and microwave on HIGH for 5–7 minutes until softened, stirring frequently.

5 Stir in the liver and half the rind. Microwave on HIGH for 3–4 minutes until the liver just changes colour, stirring occasionally.

6 Stir in the satsuma segments and parsley. Microwave on HIGH for 3–4 minutes until the liver is tender and the satsumas have softened slightly.

7 Serve the liver, garnished with the remaining pared rind strips, on a bed of hot green tagliatelle.

Strips of Liver with Fresh Herbs

Serves 4
253 calories per serving

15 ml (1 tbsp) polyunsaturated oil

2 medium onions, skinned and sliced

450 g (1 lb) lamb's or calf's liver, sliced

100 g (4 oz) button mushrooms, sliced

30 ml (2 tbsp) chopped fresh mixed herbs, such as parsley, sage, tarragon

10 ml (2 level tsp) Dijon mustard

salt and pepper

fresh herb sprigs, to garnish

Use lamb's liver for a family meal and calf's liver, considered the finest, for a special occasion. Although lamb's liver has a good flavour and texture, it is slightly coarser and darker than calf's.

1 Put the oil in a shallow dish and microwave on HIGH for 30 seconds. Stir in the onion and microwave on HIGH for 7 minutes until tender and softened, stirring occasionally.

2 Meanwhile, cut the liver lengthways into pencil-thin strips, trimming away all ducts and gristle.

3 Add the liver to the dish and microwave on HIGH for 3–4 minutes until the liver just changes colour, stirring occasionally.

4 Stir in the mushrooms, herbs and mustard, and season with salt and pepper to taste. Cover, leaving a gap to let steam escape, and microwave on HIGH for 4–5 minutes until the liver is tender. Serve hot, garnish with sprigs of fresh herbs.

Provençal Pork Fillet

Serves 4
236 calories per serving

2 medium courgettes, trimmed

397 g (14 oz) can tomatoes

1 garlic clove, skinned and crushed

1 medium onion, skinned and finely chopped

15 ml (1 level tbsp) tomato purée

60 ml (4 tbsp) dry red wine

1 bay leaf

fresh thyme sprig or pinch dried

few basil leaves or pinch dried

salt and pepper

450 g (1 lb) pork fillet

15 ml (1 tbsp) polyunsaturated oil

Serve these lean slices of pork fillet, cooked in a mouthwatering sauce of courgettes, garlic, tomato, herbs and red wine, with brown rice and a green salad.

1 Cut the courgettes into 1 cm (½ inch) slices. Put in a large bowl with the tomatoes and juice, garlic, onion, tomato purée, wine, herbs and salt and pepper.

2 Cover, leaving a gap to let steam escape, and microwave on HIGH for 10 minutes, stirring once or twice during the cooking time.

3 Meanwhile, cut the pork into 1 cm (½ inch) slices. Cover with a piece of greaseproof paper and flatten them with a rolling pin.

4 Heat a large browning dish on HIGH for 5–8 minutes or according to manufacturer's instructions.

5 When the browning dish is ready, add the oil then quickly add the pork. Microwave on HIGH for 2 minutes or until lightly browned on one side.

6 Turn the pork over and microwave on HIGH for 1–2 minutes or until the second side is brown.

7 Add the cooked sauce to the dish, stirring to loosen any sediment at the bottom of the dish.

8 Microwave on HIGH for 3–4 minutes until the pork is tender, stirring occasionally. Serve hot with brown rice and a green salad.

Sweetbreads with Peppers and Fresh Herbs

Serves 4
208 calories per serving

450 g (1 lb) lamb's sweetbreads, soaked in cold water for 2 hours

juice of $\frac{1}{2}$ lemon

15 ml (1 tbsp) polyunsaturated oil

1 medium onion, skinned and thinly sliced

1 garlic clove, skinned and crushed

1 green pepper, seeded and cut into strips

1 yellow pepper, seeded and cut into strips

150 ml ($\frac{1}{4}$ pint) boiling chicken stock

10 ml (2 tsp) chopped fresh parsley

10 ml (2 tsp) snipped fresh chives

30 ml (2 tbsp) Greek strained yogurt

salt and pepper

When buying sweetbreads, they should be moist and fresh-looking. They have a delicate flavour and are easily digested.

1 Drain and rinse the sweetbreads. Pierce each sweetbread in several places to prevent them splitting during cooking. Put in a large bowl, cover with cold water and add the lemon juice.

2 Cover, leaving a gap to let steam escape, and microwave on HIGH for 7–10 minutes until boiling. Plunge into cold water to firm the meat. Remove as much membrane as possible, then cut into thick slices.

3 Put the oil, onion, garlic and peppers in a large bowl. Cover, leaving a gap to let steam escape, and microwave on HIGH for 5–7 minutes until softened, stirring occasionally.

4 With a slotted spoon, spoon the vegetables on to an ovenproof serving dish.

5 Add the sweetbreads and stock to the bowl. Re-cover and microwave on HIGH for 5–7 minutes, stirring occasionally.

6 Remove the sweetbreads with a slotted spoon and arrange on top of the vegetables. Stir the parsley, chives and yogurt into the liquid remaining in the bowl. Season with salt and pepper to taste. Microwave on HIGH for about 5 minutes until the sauce reduces by half.

7 Spoon the sauce over the sweetbreads and microwave on HIGH for 2 minutes to reheat. Serve hot.

Kidney and Courgette Kebabs

Serves 2
170 calories per serving

4 lamb's kidneys

2 medium courgettes, trimmed

15 ml (1 tbsp) polyunsaturated oil

1 garlic clove, skinned and crushed

30 ml (2 tbsp) chopped fresh parsley

5 ml (1 tsp) lemon juice

pepper

Kidneys are an excellent source of iron and surprisingly low in fat, a high proportion of which is polyunsaturated.

1 Skin the kidneys, cut each one in half lengthways and snip out the cores with scissors. Cut each in half again widthways.

2 Cut the courgettes into 1 cm ($\frac{1}{2}$ inch) slices. Thread the kidney pieces and courgettes on to four wooden skewers.

3 Put the oil and garlic in a shallow rectangular dish. Microwave on HIGH for 1–1$\frac{1}{2}$ minutes until softened. Stir in the parsley, lemon juice and pepper to taste. Microwave on HIGH for 1 minute, stirring once.

4 Arrange the kebabs in the garlic dressing. Cover loosely with a double thickness of absorbent kitchen paper. Microwave on HIGH for 6–7 minutes or until the kidneys are tender, turning them over once during cooking.

5 Transfer the kebabs to a warmed serving dish. Reheat the cooking liquid on HIGH for 2–3 minutes until reduced and slightly thickened. Serve two kebabs each with the garlic dressing poured over.

Chicken in Mustard and Lemon Sauce

Serves 4
198 calories per serving

4 chicken breasts, skinned

20 ml (4 level tsp) wholegrain mustard

juice of 1 small lemon

150 ml ($\frac{1}{4}$ pint) low-fat natural yogurt

lemon slices, to garnish

This tangy, low-fat chicken dish uses a few simple ingredients, takes only eleven minutes to cook yet produces delicious results.

1 Arrange the chicken in a single layer in a shallow dish. Spread the mustard equally on each. Sprinkle over the lemon juice.

2 Cover, leaving a gap to let steam escape, and microwave on HIGH for 8–10 minutes or until tender. Reposition the chicken once during cooking. Transfer the chicken to a warmed serving dish.

3 Stir the yogurt into the cooking dish and microwave on HIGH for 1–1$\frac{1}{2}$ minutes until heated through, stirring once. Pour over the chicken and serve hot, garnished with lemon slices. Serve with brown rice or potatoes cooked in their skins.

Coriander Chicken with Mango Sauce

Serves 4
207 calories per serving

4 chicken breasts, boned and skinned

45 ml (3 tbsp) chopped fresh coriander

75 ml (5 tbsp) dry white wine

1 small ripe mango

juice of 1 lime

salt and pepper

fresh coriander sprigs, to garnish

This unusual chicken dish, flavoured with delicately scented fresh coriander, is ideal for a small summer dinner party, accompanied by thin French beans and tiny new potatoes. When choosing the mango for the sauce, buy a golden or red one; if still a little green, allow to ripen in a warm room.

1 Using a sharp knife, make three slashes across each chicken breast. Stuff the slashes with the chopped coriander.

2 Arrange the chicken breasts in a large shallow dish and pour the wine around the chicken. Cover, leaving a gap to let steam escape, and microwave on HIGH for 10 minutes or until tender.

3 With a slotted spoon, remove the chicken breasts to a plate and set aside. Pour the juices into a blender or food processor. Peel the mango, remove the stone and add the flesh to the chicken juices with the lime juice. Blend until completely smooth. Season with salt and pepper to taste, then pour into an ovenproof serving dish.

4 Place the chicken breasts in the sauce. Cover, leaving a gap to let steam escape, and microwave on HIGH for 3 minutes or until heated through.

5 To serve, spoon a little sauce on to individual serving plates and lay a chicken breast on top. Garnish with sprigs of fresh coriander.

Chicken with Chicory and Apple

Serves 4
238 calories per serving

4 chicken breasts, skinned

15 ml (1 tbsp) polyunsaturated oil

1 small onion, skinned and thinly sliced

1 garlic clove, skinned and crushed

2 chicory heads

2 red eating apples

10 ml (2 tsp) lemon juice

150 ml ($\frac{1}{4}$ pint) low-fat natural yogurt

salt and pepper

apple slices, to garnish

The unusual combination of ingredients in this dish results in a delicious subtle flavour. Choose firm heads of white chicory, as green colouring indicates bitterness and browning is a sign of age.

1 Cut the chicken into bite-sized pieces and put in a shallow dish with the oil, onion and garlic. Cover, leaving a gap to let steam escape, and microwave on HIGH for 6–7 minutes until the chicken is tender, stirring occasionally.

2 Meanwhile, cut the chicory into 2.5 cm (1 inch) slices. Slice the apples, discarding the cores, and toss in the lemon juice.

3 Stir the chicory and apple into the chicken. Microwave on HIGH for 2–3 minutes until softened slightly.

4 Stir in the yogurt and season with salt and pepper to taste. Microwave on HIGH for 1–2 minutes or until heated through, stirring once. Serve hot, garnished with apple slices.

Chicken and Prune Kebabs

Serves 4
260 calories per serving

16 prunes, stoned

75 ml (5 tbsp) chicken stock

1 small garlic clove, skinned and crushed

15 ml (1 tbsp) dry sherry

4 chicken breast fillets, skinned and cut into 2.5 cm (1 inch) cubes

15 ml (1 tbsp) polyunsaturated oil

450 g (1 lb) leeks, trimmed and thinly sliced

30 ml (2 tbsp) smetana

salt and pepper

chopped fresh parsley, to garnish

The combination of chicken and prunes is delicious. Other dried fruits, such as apricots, could be used instead of the prunes. The kebabs are cooked and served on a bed of leeks.

1 Put the prunes, chicken stock, garlic and sherry in a medium bowl. Cover, leaving a gap to let steam escape, and microwave on HIGH for 2 minutes to plump the prunes.

2 Stir in the chicken and mix thoroughly together. Set aside while cooking the leeks.

3 Put the oil and leeks in a large shallow dish and stir to coat the leeks in the oil. Cover, leaving a gap to let steam escape, and microwave on HIGH for 10–12 minutes until the leeks are really tender, stirring occasionally.

4 Meanwhile, thread the chicken and prunes on to eight wooden skewers. Place the kebabs on top of the leeks. Cover, leaving a gap to let steam escape, and microwave on HIGH for 5–7 minutes until the chicken is tender, repositioning once.

5 Stir the smetana into the leeks and season with salt and pepper to taste. Spoon on to four warmed serving plates, then arrange two kebabs on each plate. Garnish with chopped parsley and serve immediately.

Spiced Chicken with Papaya

Serves 4
272 calories per serving

1 small ripe papaya

25 g (1 oz) creamed coconut

150 ml ($\frac{1}{4}$ pint) hot chicken stock

150 ml ($\frac{1}{4}$ pint) low-fat natural yogurt

juice of 1 lime

salt and pepper

15 ml (1 tbsp) polyunsaturated oil

1 medium onion, skinned and finely sliced

1 garlic clove, skinned and crushed

5 ml (1 level tsp) mild curry powder

4 chicken breasts, skinned

This recipe uses a fully ripe papaya. When the fruit is ripe, the skin is yellow and the flesh gives slightly to the touch; ripe papaya bruise easily so they should be eaten immediately. In this dish, the sweetness of the papaya perfectly offsets the slight bitterness of spices.

1 Peel the papaya and cut in half. Scoop out the seeds and cut the flesh into 0.5 cm ($\frac{1}{4}$ inch) slices. Set aside.

2 Blend the coconut with a little of the hot stock to form a paste, then add the remaining stock. Pass through a nylon sieve into a bowl. Add the yogurt and lime juice and season with salt and pepper to taste. Set aside.

3 Put the oil, onion and garlic in a large shallow dish. Cover, leaving a gap to let steam escape, and microwave on HIGH for 5–7 minutes until softened, stirring occasionally. Stir in the curry powder and microwave for a further 1 minute, stirring once.

4 Add the chicken breasts in a single layer and re-cover. Microwave on HIGH for 5–7 minutes.

5 Pour the prepared sauce over the chicken and re-cover. Microwave on HIGH for 2 minutes until hot.

6 Add the papaya and re-cover. Microwave for a further 2 minutes until hot and the chicken is tender. Serve with brown rice.

Groundnut Stew

Serves 4
375 calories per serving

15 ml (1 tbsp) polyunsaturated oil

15 ml (1 level tbsp) paprika

5 ml (1 level tsp) ground cumin

2.5 ml (½ level tsp) chilli powder

100 g (4 oz) shelled unsalted peanuts

4 chicken breast fillets, skinned

30 ml (2 tbsp) shoyu sauce

1 garlic clove, skinned and crushed

1 fresh green chilli, seeded and chopped (optional)

3 large tomatoes, chopped

grated rind and juice of 1 lime

Peanuts are called groundnuts in West Africa, where this dish originally came from. Substitute 350 g (12 oz) turkey fillet for the chicken, if preferred.

1 Put the oil, paprika, cumin, chilli and peanuts into a shallow dish. Microwave on HIGH for 5 minutes, stirring occasionally. Set aside.

2 Cut the chicken into 2.5 cm (1 inch) cubes and place in a medium bowl with the shoyu sauce and garlic. Cover, leaving a gap to let steam escape, and microwave on HIGH for 5 minutes.

3 Meanwhile, put the peanut mixture, chilli, if used, tomatoes, lime rind and juice, if used, and 150 ml (¼ pint) water in a blender or food processor and purée until almost smooth.

4 Add the chicken and stir well to mix. Microwave on HIGH for 5–7 minutes or until the chicken is very tender, stirring occasionally. Serve hot, with brown rice.

Devilled Chicken

Serves 4
406 calories per serving

30 ml (2 level tbsp) Dijon or made mustard

15 ml (1 level tbsp) paprika

15 ml (1 level tbsp) ground turmeric

15 ml (1 level tbsp) ground cumin

30 ml (2 level tbsp) tomato purée

45 ml (3 tbsp) lemon juice

15 g (½ oz) polyunsaturated margarine

4 chicken quarters, each weighing about 350 g (12 oz)

15 ml (1 tbsp) poppy seeds

This spicy dish is quite hot but if you would like it hotter, add a few drops of Tabasco sauce to the mustard paste.

1 Put the mustard, paprika, turmeric, cumin, tomato purée, lemon juice and margarine in a small bowl and beat well to make a thick smooth paste.

2 Using a sharp knife, remove any excess fat from the chicken quarters and make several slashes in the skin. Spread the paste evenly over the chicken and sprinkle with the poppy seeds. Arrange in a single layer in a large shallow flameproof serving dish.

3 Cover, leaving a gap to let steam escape, and microwave on HIGH for 12–15 minutes or until the chicken is tender, repositioning the chicken once.

4 Place under a preheated grill and cook for 3–4 minutes until the skin is well browned and crisp. Garnish with lemon wedges and serve hot with a crisp, mixed salad.

CHICKEN AND PRUNE KEBABS (PAGE 94)

Shredded Chicken and Vegetables with Cashew Nuts

Serves 4
296 calories per serving

75 g (3 oz) cashew nuts

3 chicken breast fillets, skinned

1 large red pepper, seeded

2 medium carrots, scrubbed

4 spring onions, trimmed

½ cucumber

½ head of Chinese leaves

30 ml (2 tbsp) shoyu sauce

1 garlic clove, skinned and crushed

10 ml (2 tsp) clear honey

1 cm (½ inch) piece fresh root ginger, peeled and grated

15 ml (1 level tbsp) black bean sauce

Make sure that the chicken and vegetables are all cut to the same size to ensure even cooking.

1 Put the cashew nuts on a large flat ovenproof plate. Microwave on HIGH for 5 minutes, stirring once. Set aside.

2 Meanwhile, cut the chicken, pepper, carrots, onions, cucumber and Chinese leaves into thin shreds no more than 0.5 cm (¼ inch) wide.

3 Place the shredded chicken and carrots in a large bowl with the shoyu sauce, garlic, honey, ginger and black bean sauce. Cover, leaving a gap to let steam escape, and microwave on HIGH for 5–6 minutes or until the chicken is tender, stirring once.

4 Add the remaining ingredients and the cashew nuts. Re-cover and microwave on HIGH for 2 minutes or until heated through. Serve immediately with noodles.

Turkey with Mushrooms

Serves 4–6
186–124 calories per serving

450 g (1 lb) turkey fillet or skinned chicken breast fillets, cut into thin strips

350 g (12 oz) button mushrooms, sliced

1–2 garlic cloves, skinned and crushed

150 ml (¼ pint) Greek strained yogurt

30 ml (2 tbsp) chopped fresh parsley

salt and pepper

parsley, to garnish

This simple, no-fuss turkey dish uses Greek strained yogurt to provide a creamy sauce. Strained yogurt is much smoother, creamier and sweeter than ordinary natural yogurt.

1 Put the turkey, mushrooms and garlic in a shallow ovenproof serving dish. Cover, leaving a gap to let steam escape, and microwave on HIGH for 7–9 minutes or until the chicken is tender, stirring occasionally.

2 Stir in the yogurt and parsley and season with salt and pepper to taste. Garnish with chopped parsley and serve immediately with brown rice or noodles.

TOP: OKRA WITH BABY ONIONS AND CORIANDER (PAGE 102)
BOTTOM: BABY CARROTS WITH WATERCRESS AND ORANGE (PAGE 104)

Cold Turkey in Hazelnut Sauce

Serves 4
312 calories per serving

4 turkey escalopes, each weighing about 175 g (6 oz)

juice of ½ lemon

30 ml (2 tbsp) chopped fresh mixed herbs, such as mint, parsley, coriander

50 g (2 oz) hazelnuts

juice of 1 lime

25 g (1 oz) creamed coconut

pinch of ground cinnamon

1 medium onion, skinned and finely chopped

1 garlic clove, skinned and crushed

150 ml (¼ pint) low-fat natural yogurt

chopped fresh herbs, to garnish

Turkey combines beautifully with this hazelnut and yogurt sauce. This mouthwatering recipe is ideal to serve on a warm summer's day.

1 Prick the turkey escalopes all over with a fork then arrange in a shallow dish in a single layer. Sprinkle with the lemon juice and herbs.

2 Cover, leaving a gap to let steam escape, and microwave on HIGH for 6–7 minutes until tender.

3 Spread out the hazelnuts evenly on a large flat plate. Microwave on HIGH for 3–4 minutes or until the skins burst, stirring occasionally.

4 Rub off the skins, using a clean tea-towel, and put in a blender or food processor. Add 60 ml (4 tbsp) water, the lime juice, coconut, cinnamon, onion and garlic and work until smooth.

5 Put the hazelnut mixture into a medium bowl, cover, leaving a gap to let steam escape, and microwave on HIGH for 4–5 minutes. Leave to cool for 2–3 minutes, then stir in the yogurt. Pour the hazelnut sauce over the cooked turkey. Chill for 2–3 hours before serving. Garnish.

Quail with Lemon and Chervil

Serves 2
154 calories per serving

15 ml (1 tbsp) olive oil

4 quail, cleaned

2 medium carrots, thinly sliced

60 ml (4 tbsp) dry white wine

juice of 1 small lemon

150 ml (¼ pint) chicken stock

salt and pepper

10 ml (2 tsp) chopped fresh chervil or 5 ml (1 level tsp) dried

chervil sprigs, to garnish

Quail, traditionally classed as game birds, are low in polyunsaturated fat.

1 Heat a large browning dish on HIGH for 5–8 minutes or according to manufacturer's instructions.

2 Add the oil to the dish, add the quail, breast side down and microwave on HIGH for 2 minutes. Turn them over and microwave for 1 minute.

3 Add the carrots, wine, lemon juice and hot stock. Cover, leaving a gap to let steam escape, and microwave on HIGH for 6–8 minutes or until tender, turning the quail once during cooking.

4 With a slotted spoon, transfer the quail and carrots to a warmed serving dish. Microwave the cooking liquid on HIGH for 3–4 minutes or until reduced by half. Season and stir in the chervil. Serve two quail each on a bed of carrots. Pour over the sauce, garnish and serve.

CHAPTER 8

Accompaniments

Sliced Potatoes with Cheese and Mustard

Serves 4–6
170–113 calories per serving

225 g (8 oz) onions, skinned
and thinly sliced

450 g (1 lb) potatoes, skinned
and thinly sliced

150 ml (¼ pint) low-fat natural
yogurt

15 ml (1 level tbsp)
wholegrain mustard

salt and pepper

25 g (1 oz) Cheddar cheese,
grated

Use a wholegrain variety of mustard for this tempting potato dish; there are plenty to choose from in larger supermarkets. Wholegrain mustard is fairly hot and peps up all kinds of foods.

1 Put the onions and 15 ml (1 tbsp) water in a shallow 1.1 litre (2 pint) ovenproof serving dish. Cover, leaving a gap to let steam escape, and microwave on HIGH for 3 minutes.

2 Add the potatoes, mixing gently with the onions. Whisk together the yogurt, mustard and salt and pepper to taste, and pour over the potatoes.

3 Re-cover, then microwave on HIGH for 15 minutes until the potatoes are tender.

4 Sprinkle the grated cheese over the top. Microwave on HIGH for 1–2 minutes until the cheese has melted. Serve hot.

Marinated Aubergine Salad

Serves 4
95 calories per serving

2 medium aubergines, total
weight about 550 g (1¼ lb)

30 ml (2 tbsp) sesame oil

15 ml (1 tbsp) wine vinegar

10 ml (2 tsp) shoyu sauce

1 medium green pepper, seeded
and thinly sliced

2 garlic cloves, skinned and
crushed

2.5 cm (1 inch) piece of fresh
root ginger, peeled and grated

5 ml (1 tsp) sweet chilli sauce

15 ml (1 level tbsp) sesame
seeds

Flavoured with ginger, garlic, chilli and shoyu, this chilled aubergine dish is reminiscent of an oriental salad. It should be made the day before serving and is delicious with barbecued meats.

1 Rub the aubergines with 5 ml (1 tsp) of the oil, prick well all over with a fork and place on a double thickness of absorbent kitchen paper. Microwave on HIGH for 6 minutes. Turn over and microwave on HIGH for a further 6–8 minutes or until the aubergines are soft. Set aside.

2 Meanwhile, put 15 ml (1 tbsp) of the oil, the vinegar and shoyu sauce in a bowl and whisk together. Set aside.

3 Put the remaining oil in a medium bowl and add the green pepper, garlic and ginger. Cover, leaving a gap to let steam escape, and microwave on HIGH for 2–3 minutes. The pepper should soften slightly but still be crisp.

4 Add the dressing and stir well together. Microwave on HIGH for a further 1 minute.

5 Cut the aubergines into 2.5 cm (1 inch) cubes and put in a serving bowl. Add the chilli sauce and the green pepper and dressing and toss together. Allow to cool then chill before serving sprinkled with the sesame seeds.

French Beans with Onion and Mint

Serves 4
88 calories per serving

15 ml (1 tbsp) polyunsaturated oil

1 large onion, skinned and very thinly sliced

450 g (1 lb) French beans, trimmed and halved

15 ml (1 tbsp) white wine vinegar

30 ml (2 tbsp) Greek strained yogurt

30 ml (2 tbsp) chopped fresh mint

salt and pepper

Serve this vegetable accompaniment hot in winter, cold in summer.

1 Put the oil and onion in a large ovenproof serving dish and mix together so that the onions are coated in oil. Cover, leaving a gap to let steam escape, and microwave on HIGH for 7–8 minutes until tender.

2 Add the beans, re-cover and microwave on HIGH for 3–4 minutes until the beans are just tender, stirring occasionally.

3 Stir in the vinegar, yogurt and mint. Season with salt and pepper to taste and toss together to mix. Serve hot or cold.

Hot Shredded Celeriac and Carrot

Serves 4
38 calories per serving

450 g (1 lb) celeriac, peeled

30 ml (2 tbsp) lemon juice

2 large carrots, scrubbed and trimmed

salt and pepper

30 ml (2 tbsp) snipped fresh chives

Celeriac is a knobbly root vegetable with a flavour similar to celery. It combines particularly well with carrot to provide this unusual, yet simple to prepare, low-calorie vegetable accompaniment.

1 Coarsely grate the celeriac into a large bowl. Add the lemon juice and 30 ml (2 tbsp) water and toss together to prevent discoloration. Coarsely grate the carrots and mix with the celeriac.

2 Cover, leaving a gap to let steam escape, and microwave on HIGH for 10–12 minutes until tender, stirring occasionally.

3 Season with salt and pepper to taste and serve sprinkled with the chopped chives.

Vegetables Julienne

Serves 4
27 calories per serving

4 medium courgettes, trimmed

4 medium carrots, scrubbed

1 red pepper, seeded

15 ml (1 tbsp) lemon juice

salt and pepper

Julienne is a French description of a food cut into matchstick shapes. Vegetables cut this way make an elegant dish.

1 Cut the courgettes, carrots and red pepper into neat julienne strips 5 cm (2 inches) long and 0.5 cm ($\frac{1}{4}$ inch) wide.

2 Put the vegetables and lemon juice in an ovenproof serving dish. Cover, leaving a gap to let steam escape, and microwave on HIGH for 5–7 minutes or until the vegetables are just tender.

3 Season with salt and pepper to taste and serve immediately.

Chinese Cabbage with Ginger

Serves 6
35 calories per serving

4 cm (1$\frac{1}{2}$ inch) piece fresh root ginger, peeled and thinly sliced

15 ml (1 tbsp) olive oil

15 ml (1 tbsp) shoyu sauce

large pinch of ground cloves

1 head of Chinese cabbage, trimmed and coarsely shredded

salt and pepper

Chinese cabbage is also known as Chinese leaves. It has tightly packed leaves with a sweet taste and crisp texture and it makes an excellent alternative to cabbage when cooked or lettuce if left raw.

1 Put the ginger, oil, shoyu sauce and cloves in an ovenproof serving dish. Microwave on HIGH for 2 minutes, stirring once.

2 Stir in the Chinese cabbage and stir to coat in the oil. Season with salt and pepper to taste. Microwave on HIGH for 3–4 minutes until hot but still crunchy, stirring once. Serve immediately.

Okra with Baby Onions and Coriander

Serves 4–6
65–43 calories per serving

15 ml (1 tbsp) olive oil

15 ml (1 tbsp) coriander seeds, crushed

1 garlic clove, skinned and crushed

225 g (8 oz) baby onions, skinned and halved

450 g (1 lb) okra, trimmed

Okra are green ribbed pods with white flesh and edible seeds. They are often referred to as 'ladies' fingers' because of their long tapering shape. When trimming the ends before cooking, take care not to cut into the flesh or a sticky substance will be released during cooking.

1 Put the oil, coriander and garlic in an ovenproof serving bowl. Microwave on HIGH for 2 minutes, stirring once.

2 Add the onions, okra and stock and mix well together. Cover, leaving a gap to let steam escape,

30 ml (2 tbsp) vegetable stock

salt and pepper

and microwave on HIGH for 5–7 minutes until the onions and okra are tender, stirring occasionally. Season with salt and pepper to taste and serve immediately.

Courgettes Tossed in Parmesan Cheese

Serves 4
75 calories per serving

450 g (1 lb) courgettes, trimmed

15 ml (1 tbsp) olive oil

1–2 garlic cloves, skinned and crushed

salt and pepper

25 g (1 oz) fresh Parmesan cheese, grated

Use grated, fresh Parmesan cheese in this recipe. The grated Parmesan sold in cartons has an unpleasant bitter taste and is no substitute.

1 Cut the courgettes into 0.5 cm ($\frac{1}{4}$ inch) slices.

2 Put the oil and garlic in a medium bowl. Microwave on HIGH for 2–3 minutes until lightly browned, stirring occasionally.

3 Add the courgettes and toss to coat in the oil. Cover, leaving a gap to let steam escape, and microwave on HIGH for about 4 minutes until the courgettes are just tender, stirring frequently.

4 Season with salt and pepper to taste and sprinkle in the Parmesan cheese. Toss together until mixed then serve hot.

Green and White Cabbage with Poppy Seeds

Serves 4–6
24–16 calories per serving

225 g (8 oz) green cabbage, finely shredded

225 g (8 oz) white cabbage, finely shredded

30 ml (2 tbsp) vegetable stock

15 ml (1 tbsp) poppy seeds

salt and pepper

freshly grated nutmeg

It is difficult to over-cook cabbage in the microwave, and the crisp and green result of this recipe, makes it an attractive low-calorie accompaniment.

1 Put the cabbage and vegetable stock in a large ovenproof serving bowl. Cover, leaving a gap to let steam escape, and microwave on HIGH for 6–8 minutes or until softened but still crunchy, stirring occasionally.

2 Add the poppy seeds and season with salt, pepper and freshly grated nutmeg to taste. Serve immediately.

Turned Vegetables in Lemon Sauce

Serves 4
116 calories per serving

3 medium potatoes, peeled

4 medium carrots, scrubbed

grated rind and juice of ½ small lemon

30 ml (2 tbsp) smetana or Greek strained yogurt

salt and pepper

chopped fresh parsley, to garnish

Preparing turned potatoes and carrots is time consuming but well worth the effect for a special occasion.

1 Trim the potatoes and carrots flat at both ends. Cut the potatoes into quarters and the carrots in half widthways. With a small, sharp knife, trim each piece into elongated trunks then trim each trunk into a six-sided barrel shape.

2 Put the prepared vegetables in a medium bowl and add the lemon rind and juice and 15 ml (1 tbsp) water.

3 Cover, leaving a gap to let steam escape, and microwave on HIGH for about 7–8 minutes until the vegetables are tender.

4 Uncover and stir in the smetana. Microwave on HIGH for a further minute until the sauce has thickened slightly.

5 Season with salt and pepper to taste and serve garnished with chopped parsley.

Baby Carrots with Watercress and Orange

Serves 4
60 calories per serving

bunch of watercress

450 g (1 lb) whole new carrots, scrubbed

15 g (½ oz) polyunsaturated margarine

60 ml (4 tbsp) orange juice

salt and pepper

Orange and watercress, both rich in vitamin C, are a perfect combination with sweet, baby carrots. Watercress is also a good source of iron.

1 Wash the watercress and reserve a few sprigs to garnish. Cut away any coarse stalks. Chop the leaves and remaining stalks.

2 Put the watercress and carrots in a shallow dish. Dot the margarine over the vegetables and spoon over the orange juice. Season with pepper only.

3 Cover, leaving a gap to let steam escape, and microwave on HIGH for 10–12 minutes or until tender. Adjust the seasoning before serving.

Parsley Purée

Serves 4
92 calories per serving

15 ml (1 tbsp) polyunsaturated oil

1 garlic clove, skinned and crushed

1 medium onion, skinned and finely chopped

50 g (2 oz) fresh parsley, roughly chopped

15 ml (1 tbsp) lemon juice

150 ml ($\frac{1}{4}$ pint) Greek strained yogurt

salt and pepper

Parsley is not often served as a vegetable accompaniment which makes this recipe slightly unusual. However, not only is it delicious, it is also good for you as parsley contains large quantities of vitamins A, B and C, iron and other essential minerals. The purée has a pronounced flavour and should therefore be served in small quantities.

1 Put the oil, garlic and onion in a medium bowl. Cover, leaving a gap to let steam escape, and microwave on HIGH for 5–7 minutes until softened, stirring occasionally.

2 Stir in the parsley and lemon juice. Re-cover and microwave on HIGH for 2 minutes until soft, stirring occasionally.

3 Stir in the yogurt and microwave on HIGH for 1 minute until hot. Season with salt and pepper to taste and serve immediately.

Herby Rice Pilaff

Serves 4–6
205–137 calories per serving

1 medium onion, skinned and finely chopped

1 garlic clove, skinned and crushed

450 ml ($\frac{3}{4}$ pint) boiling vegetable or chicken stock

225 g (8 oz) long-grain brown rice

salt and pepper

60 ml (4 tbsp) chopped fresh herbs, such as parsley, tarragon, marjoram, chives, chervil

When serving this well-flavoured brown rice pilaff with a main course dish, choose herbs that complement the main dish. Dried herbs will not give the same fresh flavour.

1 Put the onion, garlic, stock and rice into a large bowl. Cover, leaving a gap to let steam escape, and microwave on HIGH for 30–35 minutes or until tender, stirring once and adding a little extra water if necessary. Leave to stand, covered, for 5 minutes, by which time all the water should be absorbed.

2 Season with salt and pepper to taste, and mix in the herbs lightly with a fork. Serve immediately.

Saffron Rice with Chick Peas

Serves 4
220 calories per serving

100 g (4 oz) chick peas, soaked overnight and drained

1 small onion, skinned and finely chopped

1 garlic clove, skinned and crushed

large pinch of saffron strands

900 ml (1½ pints) boiling vegetable stock

100 g (4 oz) long-grain brown rice

150 ml (¼ pint) low-fat natural yogurt

15 ml (1 level tbsp) grated fresh Parmesan cheese

salt and pepper

Protein-rich chick peas and brown rice make an interesting combination of tastes and textures, and are a substantial accompaniment.

1 Put the chick peas, onion, garlic and saffron in a large bowl. Pour over 450 ml (¾ pint) of the stock and stir. Cover, leaving a gap to let steam escape, and microwave on HIGH for 15 minutes.

2 Add the rice and remaining stock. Re-cover and microwave on HIGH for 30–35 minutes until the chick peas are tender.

3 Meanwhile, mix the yogurt and cheese together and season with salt and pepper to taste. Pour the dressing over the chick peas and rice and toss together to mix. Leave to stand for 5 minutes before serving.

Lentil, Rice and Watercress Salad

Serves 6
150 calories per serving

100 g (4 oz) green lentils

100 g (4 oz) long-grain brown rice

2 bay leaves

strip of lemon rind

15 ml (1 level tbsp) wholegrain mustard

30 ml (2 tbsp) lemon juice

100 g (4 oz) cottage cheese

½ small bunch of watercress, trimmed and finely chopped

salt and pepper

few watercress sprigs, to garnish

Cottage cheese and watercress are used to make up the unusual dressing for this filling salad which also contains green lentils and brown rice.

1 Put the lentils, rice, bay leaves and lemon rind in a medium bowl. Pour over 1.1 litres (2 pints) boiling water. Cover, leaving a gap to let steam escape, and microwave on HIGH for 30–35 minutes or until the lentils and rice are tender. Leave to stand for 5 minutes while making the dressing.

2 To make the dressing, put the mustard into a small bowl and gradually whisk in the lemon juice, cottage cheese and watercress. Season with salt and pepper to taste.

3 Drain the lentils and rice and rinse with boiling water. Discard the lemon rind and bay leaves. Turn into a serving bowl, pour over the dressing and toss thoroughly together. Garnish with watercress. Serve while still warm or leave to cool and serve cold.

Barley and Mushroom Pilaff

Serves 4–6
237–158 calories per serving

25 g (1 oz) flaked almonds

175 g (6 oz) pot barley

450 ml ($\frac{3}{4}$ pint) boiling vegetable stock

100 g (4 oz) mushrooms, thinly sliced

25 g (1 oz) sultanas

10 ml (2 tsp) olive oil

30 ml (2 tbsp) chopped fresh parsley or mint

salt and pepper

Pot barley contains more B vitamins, minerals and fibre than refined pearl barley as only the rough outer husk of the grain has been removed. It makes an interesting alternative to rice in pilaffs.

1 Put the almonds on an ovenproof plate. Microwave on HIGH for 5–6 minutes until lightly browned. Set aside.

2 Put the barley and stock in a medium bowl. Cover, leaving a gap to let steam escape, and microwave on HIGH for 25–30 minutes or until tender and most of the liquid has been absorbed.

3 Stir in the mushrooms, sultanas and oil and mix together. Re-cover and microwave on HIGH for 2–3 minutes or until the mushrooms are tender.

4 Stir in the almonds and parsley or mint and season with salt and pepper to taste. Leave to stand for 5 minutes, then serve immediately.

Wholewheat and Nut Salad

Serves 6
243 calories per serving

225 g (8 oz) wholewheat grain, soaked overnight

60 ml (4 tbsp) low-fat natural yogurt

15 ml (1 tbsp) polyunsaturated oil

30 ml (2 tbsp) lemon juice

salt and pepper

100 g (4 oz) unsalted peanuts, roughly chopped

45 ml (3 tbsp) chopped fresh mint

$\frac{1}{4}$ cucumber, diced

Wholewheat grains contain second class protein and when mixed with nuts, also a second class protein, they provide good quality protein for healthy growth and repair of body tissue.

1 Drain the wholewheat grain and put in a large bowl. Add enough boiling water to cover the wholewheat. Cover the bowl, leaving a gap to let steam escape, and microwave on HIGH for 10 minutes or until tender, stirring occasionally.

2 Meanwhile, whisk together the yogurt, oil, lemon juice and salt and pepper to taste.

3 When the wholewheat is cooked, leave to stand, covered, for a further 5 minutes. Drain off any remaining water.

4 While still warm, add the dressing to the wholewheat and toss together. Stir in the peanuts, mint and cucumber. Serve cold.

Chick Peas with Tomatoes

Serves 4
193 calories per serving

1 medium onion, skinned and finely chopped

1–2 garlic cloves, skinned and crushed

5 ml (1 level tsp) ground turmeric

10 ml (2 level tsp) ground coriander

10 ml (2 level tsp) ground cumin

5 ml (1 level tsp) paprika

2.5 ml ($\frac{1}{2}$ level tsp) mild chilli powder

10 ml (2 tsp) polyunsaturated oil

4 tomatoes, roughly chopped

450 g (1 lb) cooked chick peas or two 425 g (15 oz) cans, drained and rinsed

salt and pepper

15 ml (1 tbsp) chopped fresh mint

15 ml (1 tbsp) chopped fresh coriander

Serve this spicy side dish, hot or cold, as part of an Indian-style meal.

1 Put the onion, garlic, turmeric, coriander, cumin, paprika, chilli and oil in a medium bowl. Cover, leaving a gap to let steam escape, and microwave on HIGH for 5 minutes or until the onion is softened, stirring once.

2 Add the tomatoes and chick peas and mix well together. Microwave on HIGH for 5 minutes or until the tomatoes are very soft, stirring occasionally.

3 Season with salt and pepper to taste and stir in the mint and coriander. Serve hot or cold.

CHAPTER 9

Puddings

Date and Hazelnut Stuffed Apples

Serves 4
153 calories per serving

25 g (1 oz) stoned dates

25 g (1 oz) hazelnuts

25 g (1 oz) coarse oatmeal

4 medium cooking apples, each weighing about 225–275 g (8–10 oz)

Any fruit enclosed in a skin is likely to burst during cooking in the microwave, so it is advisable to score or pierce the skin to allow the steam to escape. The dates used here add a natural sweetness to the filling in this high-fibre pudding.

1 Roughly chop the dates and nuts and put in a bowl. Add the oatmeal and mix well together.

2 Remove the cores from the apples, then score around the middle of each to allow the steam to escape. Place the apples in a shallow dish.

3 Fill the apples with the nut mixture, piling it up if necessary. Cover, leaving a gap to let steam escape and slack enough in the centre to allow the stuffing to rise.

4 Microwave on HIGH for about 8–12 minutes or until the apples are almost tender. Turn the dish once during the cooking time. Leave to stand for 3–4 minutes before serving with low-fat natural yogurt.

Osborne Pudding

Serves 4
193 calories per serving

3 slices of wholemeal bread

25 g (1 oz) polyunsaturated margarine

45 ml (3 level tbsp) reduced-sugar marmalade

2 eggs

300 ml ($\frac{1}{2}$ pint) skimmed milk

freshly grated nutmeg

This pudding is a healthier alternative to traditional bread and butter pudding yet just as good to eat.

1 Spread the bread slices with the margarine, then with the marmalade. Cut the bread into fingers or small squares and arrange, marmalade side uppermost, in layers in a 900 ml (1$\frac{1}{2}$ pint) flameproof dish.

2 Beat the eggs together in a bowl then blend in the milk. Pour the mixture over the bread and sprinkle a little nutmeg on top. Leave to stand for about 30 minutes so that the bread absorbs some of the liquid.

3 Microwave, uncovered, on LOW for 20 minutes until just set. Leave to stand for 5 minutes. Brown the top under a preheated grill, then serve hot.

Almond-stuffed Peaches

Serves 4
140 calories per serving

4 firm ripe peaches

50 g (2 oz) ground almonds

finely grated rind of ½ orange

5 ml (1 tsp) clear honey

150 ml (¼ pint) unsweetened orange juice

15 ml (1 tbsp) Amaretto (optional)

few mint leaves, to decorate

This is a light and refreshing pudding to serve in the summer. You can use nectarines instead of peaches if you prefer.

1 Cut the peaches in half and carefully ease out the stones. Make the hollows in the peaches a little deeper with a teaspoon.

2 Finely chop the removed peach flesh and mix with the almonds, orange rind, honey and 15 ml (1 tbsp) of the orange juice.

3 Use this mixture to stuff the peach halves, mounding the filling slightly.

4 Place the peaches around the edge of a large shallow dish. Mix the remaining orange juice with the Amaretto, if using, and pour around the peaches.

5 Cover, leaving a gap to let steam escape, and microwave on HIGH for 3–5 minutes until the peaches are tender. Leave to stand for 5 minutes, then serve warm with the juices spooned over and decorated with mint leaves.

Tropical Banana and Mango

Serves 4
98 calories per serving

1 large ripe mango

2 bananas

juice of 1 lime

60 ml (4 tbsp) mango juice

30 ml (2 tbsp) coconut liqueur or rum

Mango, with its slightly fibrous texture, tastes like a cross between a peach, an apricot and a melon. Mango juice is used in this warm fruit salad and is available in small cartons.

1 Peel the mango and, using a sharp knife, cut the flesh away from the flat oval stone. Discard the stone. Cut the mango flesh into bite-size pieces and place in a shallow ovenproof serving dish.

2 Peel the bananas and cut in half, then cut in half again lengthways. Add to the mango pieces with the lime juice, mango juice and coconut liqueur. Mix well together.

3 Microwave on HIGH for 2–3 minutes until warm and the banana slightly softened, stirring once. Serve immediately.

Summer Fruit Crumble

Serves 4–6
255–170 calories per serving

225 g (8 oz) eating apples, peeled, cored and thinly sliced

350 g (12 oz) raspberries, strawberries or blackberries, hulled

25 g (1 oz) polyunsaturated margarine

50 g (2 oz) plain wholemeal flour

50 g (2 oz) rolled oats

15 ml (1 level tbsp) wheat germ

30 ml (2 level tbsp) unsweetened desiccated coconut

2.5–5 ml ($\frac{1}{2}$–1 level tsp) ground cinnamon

25 g (1 oz) chopped mixed nuts

This is a sugar-free fruit crumble using coconut and nuts for sweetness instead.

1 Arrange the fruit in a 1.1 litre (2 pint) round serving dish. Cover, leaving a gap to let steam escape, and microwave on HIGH for 4–6 minutes until the apple is softened.

2 Meanwhile, rub the margarine into the flour until the mixture resembles fine breadcrumbs. Stir in the oats, wheat germ, coconut, cinnamon and nuts and mix thoroughly together.

3 Spoon the crumble mixture over the fruit and lightly press it down. Microwave on HIGH for 5–8 minutes until the topping is firm. Leave to stand for 5 minutes, then serve hot with low-fat natural yogurt.

Poached Apples and Pears

Serves 4
82 calories per serving

300 ml ($\frac{1}{2}$ pint) dry cider

1 cinnamon stick

2 cloves

2 large eating apples

2 large firm pears

3 large fresh dates (optional)

Fruit poached in the microwave retains its shape, texture and flavour well. Cooked in cider, these spicy apple and pear slices can be served hot or cold.

1 Put the cider, cinnamon and cloves in a large ovenproof serving bowl. Microwave on HIGH for 3–5 minutes or until boiling.

2 Core and thinly slice the apples and pears and stir into the hot cider. Cover, leaving a gap to let steam escape, and microwave on HIGH for 4–5 minutes or until tender, stirring once.

3 Meanwhile, stone the dates and cut into thin slices lengthways. Sprinkle the dates on top of the poached fruit. Serve hot or cold.

ALMOND-STUFFED PEACHES (PAGE 111)

Blackberry and Apple Mousses

Serves 6
115 calories per serving

450 g (1 lb) cooking apples

juice of ½ lemon

450 g (1 lb) fresh blackberries

15 ml (1 level tbsp) gelatine

240 g (8½ oz) Greek strained yogurt

15–30 ml (1–2 tbsp) concentrated apple juice

1 egg white

Make this light, pretty dessert in the autumn when both fruits are in season. Full of flavour, blackberries (which can be picked from the hedgerows) provide the attractive colour of the mousses.

1 Peel, core and thickly slice the apples. Put in a large bowl with the lemon juice and blackberries. Reserve 12 whole blackberries for decoration.

2 Cover, leaving a gap to let steam escape, and microwave on HIGH for 5–7 minutes until the apples are soft.

3 Push the apple and blackberry mixture through a nylon sieve to form a purée. Alternatively, put in a blender or food processor and work until smooth, then push through a nylon sieve to remove the pips. Allow to cool completely.

4 In a small bowl, sprinkle the gelatine into 60 ml (4 tbsp) cold water and leave to soak for 1 minute. Microwave on LOW for 1–2 minutes until the gelatine is dissolved, stirring occasionally. Stir into the apple mixture.

5 Stir the yogurt and apple juice to taste into the apple and blackberry mixture. Whisk the egg white until stiff. Fold into the mixture.

6 Spoon the mixture into six 150 ml (¼ pint) ramekin dishes and chill overnight until set. Serve decorated with the reserved blackberries.

BLACKCURRANT JELLY WITH FRESH FRUIT (PAGE 116)

Sweet Carrot Pudding

Serves 6
163 calories per serving

450 g (1 lb) young carrots, scrubbed

450 ml (¾ pint) skimmed milk

15 ml (1 tbsp) treacle

15 ml (1 tbsp) clear honey

60 ml (4 level tbsp) fine oatmeal

50 g (2 oz) ground almonds

50 g (2 oz) sultanas

10 ml (2 tsp) orange flower water

pistachio nuts, slivered, to decorate

This unusual recipe is based on a delicious Indian pudding called Gajar Halva. Most of the sweetness comes from the carrots, so little sweetening is necessary; the dish is also high in fibre and vitamins. Challenge your family or guests to guess what it is made from!

1 Finely grate the carrots into a large bowl and stir in the milk, treacle and honey. Microwave on HIGH for 18–20 minutes until slightly reduced and thickened, and the carrots are very soft.

2 Sprinkle in the oatmeal and almonds, then beat thoroughly together. Add the sultanas and microwave on HIGH for 5 minutes until the mixture is very thick, stirring occasionally.

3 Stir in the orange flower water. Decorate with nuts and serve hot or cold.

Warm Tangerine and Kiwi Fruit Parcels

Serves 4
62 calories per serving

4 small, thin skinned seedless tangerines

3 kiwi fruit, peeled and sliced

2 passion fruit

60 ml (4 level tbsp) fromage frais

few drops of orange flower water (optional)

10 ml (2 tsp) clear honey (optional)

This is an unusual and attractive way of serving fresh fruit. When cooked, the greaseproof paper parcels of prettily arranged fruit are filled with a mixture of passion fruit and fromage frais.

1 Peel the tangerines and remove all pith. Carefully separate the segments to make a large flower shape, keeping the base still attached.

2 Cut four 30.5 cm (12 inch) squares of greaseproof paper. Arrange the kiwi fruit in a small circle on each square, leaving a hole in the middle. Place a tangerine on top of each circle of kiwi fruit. Gather the paper up around the fruit to make four parcels and twist the edges together to seal.

3 Halve the passion fruit, scoop out the seeds and mix with the fromage frais. Add a few drops of orange flower water, if using.

4 Arrange the parcels in a circle in the cooker. Microwave on HIGH for 1–2 minutes or until warm.

5 To serve, arrange on four serving plates, open the parcels slightly and place a spoonful of the fromage frais mixture in the centre of each. Drizzle with the honey and serve immediately while still warm.

Chilled Apricot Custards

Serves 3–4
150–112 calories per serving

100 g (4 oz) dried apricots

1 egg, size 2

15 ml (1 level tbsp) cornflour

225 ml (8 fl oz) skimmed milk

7 g ($\frac{1}{4}$ oz) flaked almonds

The sweet flavour of this light pudding comes from the natural sweetness of the dried apricots. They contain more protein than other dried fruits and are a good source of iron.

1 Put the apricots and 150 ml ($\frac{1}{4}$ pint) water in a small bowl. Cover, leaving a gap to let steam escape, and microwave on HIGH for 3 minutes, stirring once.

2 Leave to stand for 10 minutes, then put in a blender or food processor and work to form a purée. Set aside.

3 In a medium bowl, lightly whisk the egg then blend in the cornflour. Stir in the milk.

4 Microwave, uncovered, on HIGH for about 3 minutes until thickened, whisking every minute.

5 Stir the apricot purée into the cooked custard then turn into four individual serving dishes. Chill for at least 1 hour before serving.

6 Meanwhile, put the almonds on a large flat ovenproof plate. Microwave on HIGH for 6–8 minutes or until lightly browned, stirring occasionally. Sprinkle the almonds on top of the custards before serving.

Bitter Sweet Mousses

Serves 4
175 calories per serving

150 g (5 oz) unsweetened carob bar

15 g ($\frac{1}{2}$ oz) polyunsaturated margarine

finely grated rind and juice of 1 small orange

2 eggs, separated

orange shreds, to decorate

4 oranges, segmented, to serve

Carob is an excellent substitute for chocolate and cocoa. It tastes very similar but contains half the calories, a third of the fat and no caffeine.

1 Break the carob into small pieces and put into a medium bowl with the margarine and orange rind and juice. Microwave on HIGH for 2–3 minutes until the carob is melted, stirring occasionally.

2 Beat in the egg yolks and leave to cool for about 5 minutes.

3 Whisk the egg whites until stiff then fold into the carob mixture using a metal spoon. Pour the mixture into four 150 ml ($\frac{1}{4}$ pint) ramekin dishes, cover and chill for at least 4 hours until lightly set. Decorate with orange shreds and serve with orange segments.

Blackcurrant Jelly with Fresh Fruit

Serves 4
54 calories per serving

225 g (8 oz) blackcurrants, stringed

finely grated rind and juice of ½ lemon

15 ml (1 level tbsp) gelatine or agar-agar flakes

300 ml (½ pint) unsweetened apple juice

prepared fresh fruit in season, such as strawberries, kiwi fruit, oranges, raspberries, to serve

few mint sprigs, to decorate (optional)

Blackcurrants are rich in vitamin C. Here they are cooked lightly, without sugar, to make a dark jelly with a refreshingly sharp tang; if you prefer, add a little honey or light muscovado sugar to sweeten.

1 Put the blackcurrants and lemon rind and juice in a medium bowl. Microwave on HIGH for 5–6 minutes or until the blackcurrants are soft, stirring occasionally.

2 Put the gelatine and half of the apple juice in a small bowl. Microwave on HIGH for 1 minute until hot but not boiling.

3 Stir until dissolved then stir into the blackcurrant mixture with the remaining apple juice. If using agar-agar, proceed as before but microwave on HIGH for 1½–2 minutes until boiling.

4 Pour the jelly into four 150 ml (¼ pint) wetted moulds or ramekins and chill for 3–4 hours until set.

5 When set, turn out on to individual plates and arrange the prepared fruit attractively around the jellies. Decorate with mint sprigs, if wished.

Banana and Pistachio Cheesecakes

Serves 4
234 calories per serving

50 g (2 oz) digestive biscuits

25 g (1 oz) polyunsaturated margarine

2 medium bananas

juice of ½ lemon

225 g (8 oz) low-fat soft cheese

1 egg yolk

10 unsalted pistachio nuts, slivered, to decorate

These tempting, healthy cheesecakes have the traditional biscuit crust base. A simple way of crushing a small quantity of biscuits is to put them in a strong polythene bag and crush with a rolling pin.

1 Finely crush the biscuits and put in a bowl. Add the margarine and mix well together. Press the mixture over the bases of four 150 ml (¼ pint) ramekin dishes.

2 Mash the bananas in a bowl. Add the lemon juice, cheese and egg yolk and mix well together until smooth.

3 Spoon the mixture into the ramekin dishes and level the surface. Microwave on LOW for 15 minutes or until slightly shrinking away from the edges.

4 Leave to stand for 10 minutes, then chill for 2–3 hours. Serve decorated with the pistachio nuts.

Rolled Carob and Apricot Sponge

Serves 6–8

190–143 calories per serving

50 g (2 oz) dried apricots

30 ml (2 tbsp) orange juice

2 eggs, beaten

25 g (1 oz) dark muscovado sugar

50 g (2 oz) self-raising wholemeal flour

30 ml (2 level tbsp) carob powder

15 ml (1 tbsp) skimmed milk

300 ml ($\frac{1}{2}$ pint) Greek strained yogurt

25 g (1 oz) unsweetened carob bar

This sponge is very quick to make and is best eaten the same day. If you are counting calories, substitute the Greek strained yogurt with low-fat natural set yogurt to provide only 144–108 calories per serving.

1 Line the base of a 23 cm (9 inch) square dish with greaseproof paper.

2 Reserve one apricot for decoration, then cut the remainder into small pieces and put into a small bowl with the orange juice. Microwave on HIGH for 1 minute, to plump the apricots then set aside to cool.

3 Put the eggs and sugar into a medium bowl and whisk until pale and creamy, and thick enough to leave a trail on the surface when the whisk is lifted.

4 Sift and fold in the flour and carob powder, adding any bran left in the sieve, using a metal spoon. Fold in the milk.

5 Pour the sponge mixture into the prepared dish, level the surface and cover loosely with absorbent kitchen paper. Microwave on HIGH for $2\frac{1}{2}$–3 minutes until slightly shrunk away from the sides of the dish, but the surface still looks wet. Leave to stand for 5 minutes.

6 Meanwhile, place a sheet of greaseproof paper on a flat surface. Turn the cake out on to the greaseproof paper and roll up with the paper inside. Leave to cool on a wire rack.

7 Mix the yogurt into the orange juice and apricot mixture. Unroll the cake and spread with the filling. Reroll and place, seam side down, on a serving plate.

8 To decorate, coarsely grate the carob bar on top of the sponge roll. Cut the reserved apricot into slithers and arrange on top to decorate. Serve the rolled sponge cut into slices.

Fresh Peach Tarts

Serves 4

272 calories per serving

100 g (4 oz) plain wholemeal flour

25 g (1 oz) plain white flour

pinch of salt

50 g (2 oz) polyunsaturated margarine

3 large ripe peaches

15 ml (1 tbsp) lemon juice

75 g (3 oz) low-fat soft cheese

These delightful fruit tarts are best served soon after filling: if left completely made up for too long, the peach purée tends to soak into the pastry and make it soggy.

1 To make the pastry, put the flours and a pinch of salt into a bowl. Rub in the margarine until the mixture resembles fine breadcrumbs, then make a well in the centre and stir in 45–60 ml (3–4 tbsp) water. Mix together using a round bladed knife, then knead to give a firm, smooth dough.

2 Roll out the dough very thinly and cut out eight rounds using a 10 cm (4 inch) cutter. Use four of the rounds to line four 150 ml ($\frac{1}{4}$ pint) ramekin dishes. Prick each round several times with a fork.

3 Microwave on HIGH for 2 minutes. Turn out and leave to cool on a wire rack. Repeat with the remaining pastry rounds.

4 To make the filling, peel, halve and stone two of the peaches and purée in a blender or food processor with the lemon juice and cheese.

5 When the pastry cases are cool, spoon a little of the filling into each case. Slice the remaining peach and use to decorate the tarts.

THAWING AND COOKING CHARTS

THAWING FISH AND SHELLFISH

Separate fish cutlets, fillets or steaks as soon as possible during thawing. Like poultry, it is best to finish thawing whole fish in cold water to prevent drying out of the surface. Arrange scallops and prawns in a circle and cover with absorbent kitchen paper to help absorb liquid; remove pieces from the cooker as soon as thawed.

Type	Approximate time on LOW	Special instructions
White fish fillets or cutlets (cod, coley, haddock, halibut, or whole plaice or sole)	3–4 minutes per 450 g (1 lb) plus 2–3 minutes	*Stand* for 5 minutes after every 2 minutes.
Oily fish (whole and gutted mackerel)	2–3 minutes per 225 g (8 oz) plus 3–4 minutes	*Stand* for 5 minutes after each 2 minutes.
Kipper fillets	2–3 minutes per 225 g (8 oz)	As for oily fish above.
Lobster tails, crab claws, etc.	3–4 minutes per 225 g (8 oz) plus 2–3 minutes	As for oily fish above.
Prawns, shrimps, scampi	$2\frac{1}{2}$ minutes per 100 g (4 oz) 3–4 minutes per 225 g (8 oz)	*Pierce* plastic bag if necessary. *Stand* for 2 minutes. *Separate* with a fork after 2 minutes. *Stand* for 2 minutes, then plunge into cold water and drain.

TIME AND SETTINGS FOR COOKING FISH IN THE MICROWAVE

Type	Time/Setting	Microwave Cooking Technique(s)
Whole round fish (whiting, mullet, trout, carp, bream, small haddock)	3 minutes on HIGH per 450 g (1 lb)	*Slash* skin to prevent bursting. *Turn* over fish partway through cooking time. *Re-position* fish if cooking more than two.
Whole flat fish (plaice, sole)	3 minutes on HIGH	*Slash* skin. *Turn* dish partway through cooking time. *Shield* tail.
Cutlets, steaks, fillets	4 minutes on HIGH per 450 g (1 lb)	*Position* thicker parts towards the outside, overlapping thin ends. *Turn* over fillets and quarter-turn dish three times during cooking.

THAWING POULTRY AND GAME

Poultry or game should be thawed in its freezer wrapping which should be pierced first and the metal tag removed. During thawing, pour off liquid that collects in the bag. Finish thawing in a bowl of cold water with the bird still in its bag. Chicken portions can be thawed in their polystyrene trays.

Type	Approximate time on LOW	Special instructions
Whole chicken or duckling	6–8 minutes per 450 g (1 lb)	Remove giblets. *Stand* in cold water for 30 minutes.
Whole turkey	10–12 minutes per 450 g (1 lb)	Remove giblets. *Stand* in cold water for 2–3 hours.
Chicken portions	5–7 minutes per 450 g (1 lb)	*Separate* during thawing. *Stand* for 10 minutes.
Poussin, grouse, pheasant, pigeon, quail	5–7 minutes per 450 g (1 lb)	

TIME AND SETTINGS FOR COOKING POULTRY

Type	Time/Setting	Microwave Cooking Technique(s)
Chicken		
Whole chicken	8–10 minutes on HIGH per 450 g (1 lb)	*Cook* in a roasting bag, breast side down and turn halfway through cooking. *Stand* for 10–15 minutes.
Portions	6–8 minutes on HIGH per 450 g (1 lb)	*Position* skin side up with thinner parts towards the centre. *Re-position* halfway through cooking time. *Stand* for 5–10 minutes.
Boneless breast	2–3 minutes on HIGH	
Duck		
Whole	7–10 minutes on HIGH per 450 g (1 lb)	*Turn* over as for whole chicken. *Stand* for 10–15 minutes.
Portions	4 × 300 g (11 oz) pieces: 10 minutes on HIGH, then 30–35 minutes on MEDIUM	*Position* and *re-position* as for portions above.
Turkey		
Whole	9–11 minutes on HIGH per 450 g (1 lb)	*Turn* over three or four times, depending on size, during cooking; start cooking breast side down. *Stand* for 10–15 minutes.

THAWING MEAT

Frozen meat exudes a lot of liquid during thawing and because microwaves are attracted to water, the liquid should be poured off or mopped up with absorbent kitchen paper when it collects, otherwise thawing will take longer. Start thawing a joint in its wrapper and remove it as soon as possible—usually after one-quarter of the thawing time. Place the joint on a microwave roasting rack so that it does not stand in liquid during thawing.

Remember to turn over a large piece of meat. If the joint shows signs of cooking give the meat a 'rest' period of 20 minutes. Alternatively, shield the 'thin ends' or parts which will thaw more quickly with small, smooth pieces of foil. A joint is thawed when a skewer can easily pass through the thickest part of the meat. Chops and steaks should be re-positioned during thawing; test them by pressing the surface with your fingers—the meat should feel cold to the touch and give in the thickest part.

Do not allow the foil used for shielding to touch the sides of the oven.

Type	Approximate time on LOW	Special instructions
Beef		
Boned roasting joints (sirloin, topside)	8–10 minutes per 450 g (1 lb)	*Turn* over regularly during thawing and rest if the meat shows signs of cooking. *Stand* for 1 hour.
Joints on bone (rib of beef)	10–12 minutes per 450 g (1 lb)	*Turn* over joint during thawing. The meat will still be icy in the centre but will complete thawing if you leave it to stand for 1 hour.
Minced beef	8–10 minutes per 450 g (1 lb)	*Stand* for 10 minutes.
Cubed steak	6–8 minutes per 450 g (1 lb)	*Stand* for 10 minutes.
Steak (sirloin, rump)	8–10 minutes per 450 g (1 lb)	*Stand* for 10 minutes.
Lamb/Veal		
Boned rolled joint (loin, leg, shoulder)	5–6 minutes per 450 g (1 lb)	As for boned roasting joints of beef above. *Stand* for 30–45 minutes.
On the bone (leg and shoulder)	5–6 minutes per 450 g (1 lb)	As for beef joints on bone above. *Stand* for 30–45 minutes.
Minced lamb or veal	8–10 minutes per 450 g (1 lb)	*Stand* for 10 minutes.
Chops	8–10 minutes per 450 g (1 lb)	*Separate* during thawing. *Stand* for 10 minutes.
Pork		
Boned rolled joint (loin, leg)	7–8 minutes per 450 g (1 lb)	As for boned roasting joints of beef above. *Stand* for 1 hour.
On the bone (leg, hand)	7–8 minutes per 450 g (1 lb)	As for beef joints on bone above. *Stand* for 1 hour.
Tenderloin	8–10 minutes per 450 g (1 lb)	*Stand* for 10 minutes.
Chops	8–10 minutes per 450 g (1 lb)	*Separate* during thawing and arrange 'spoke' fashion. *Stand* for 10 minutes.

Offal

Liver	8–10 minutes per 450 g (1 lb)	*Separate* during thawing. *Stand* for 5 minutes.
Kidney	6–9 minutes per 450 g (1 lb)	*Separate* during thawing. *Stand* for 5 minutes.

TIME AND SETTINGS FOR COOKING MEAT

Type	Time/Setting	Microwave Cooking Technique(s)
Beef		
Boned roasting joint (sirloin, topside)	per 450 g (1 lb) Rare: 5–6 minutes on HIGH Medium: 7–8 minutes on HIGH Well: 8–10 minutes on HIGH	*Turn* over joint halfway through cooking time. *Stand* for 15–20 minutes, tented in foil.
On the bone roasting joint (fore rib, back rib)	per 450 g (1 lb) Rare: 5 minutes on HIGH Medium: 6 minutes on HIGH Well: 8 minutes on HIGH	*Turn* over joint halfway through cooking time. *Stand* as for boned joint.
Lamb/Veal		
Boned rolled joint (loin, leg, shoulder)	per 450 g (1 lb) Medium: 7–8 minutes on HIGH Well: 8–10 minutes on HIGH	*Turn* over joint halfway through cooking time. *Stand* as for beef.
On the bone (leg and shoulder)	per 450 g (1 lb) Medium: 6–7 minutes on HIGH Well: 8–9 minutes on HIGH	*Position* fatty side down and turn over halfway through cooking time. *Stand* as for beef.
Chops	1 chop: 2½–3½ minutes on HIGH 2 chops: 3½–4½ minutes on HIGH 3 chops: 4½–5½ minutes on HIGH 4 chops: 5½–6½ minutes on HIGH	*Cook* in preheated browning dish. *Position* with bone ends towards centre. *Turn* over once during cooking.
Bacon		
Joints	12–14 minutes on HIGH per 450 g (1 lb)	*Cook* in a pierced roasting bag. *Turn* over joint partway through cooking time. *Stand* for 10 minutes, tented in foil.
Rashers	2 rashers: 2–2½ minutes on HIGH 4 rashers: 4–4½ minutes on HIGH 6 rashers: 5–6 minutes on HIGH	*Arrange* in a single layer. *Cover* with greaseproof paper to prevent splattering. *Cook* in preheated browning dish if liked. *Remove* paper immediately after cooking to prevent sticking.

Pork

Boned rolled joint (loin, leg)	8–10 minutes on HIGH per 450 g (1 lb)	As for boned rolled lamb above.
On the bone (leg, hand)	8–9 minutes on HIGH per 450 g (1 lb)	As for lamb on the bone above.
Chops	1 chop: 4–4½ minutes on HIGH 2 chops: 5–5½ minutes on HIGH 3 chops: 6–7 minutes on HIGH 4 chops: 6½–8 minutes on HIGH	*Cook* in preheated browning dish. *Prick* kidney, if attached. *Position* with bone ends towards centre. *Turn* over once during cooking.

Offal

Liver (lamb and calves)	6–8 minutes on HIGH per 450 g (1 lb)	*Cover* with greaseproof paper to prevent splattering.
Kidneys	8 minutes on HIGH per 450 g (1 lb)	*Arrange* in a circle. *Cover* to prevent splattering. *Re-position* during cooking.

FROZEN VEGETABLES COOKING CHART

Frozen vegetables may be cooked straight from the freezer. Many may be cooked in their original plastic packaging, as long as it is first slit and then placed on a plate. Alternatively, transfer to a bowl.

Vegetable	Quantity	Approximate time on HIGH	Microwave Cooking Technique(s)
Asparagus	275 g (10 oz)	7–9 minutes	*Separate* and re-arrange after 3 minutes.
Beans, broad	225 g (8 oz)	7–8 minutes	*Stir* or *shake* during cooking period.
Beans, green cut	225 g (8 oz)	6–8 minutes	*Stir* or *shake* during cooking period.
Broccoli	275 g (10 oz)	7–9 minutes	*Re-arrange* spears after 3 minutes.
Brussels sprouts	225 g (8 oz)	6–8 minutes	*Stir* or *shake* during cooking period.
Cauliflower florets	275 g (10 oz)	7–9 minutes	*Stir* or *shake* during cooking period.
Carrots	225 g (8 oz)	6–7 minutes	*Stir* or *shake* during cooking period.
Corn-on-the-cob	1 2	3–4 minutes 6–7 minutes	*Do not* add water. Dot with butter, wrap in greaseproof paper.
Mixed vegetables	225 g (8 oz)	5–6 minutes	*Stir* or *shake* during cooking period.
Peas	225 g (8 oz)	5–6 minutes	*Stir* or *shake* during cooking period.
Peas and carrots	225 g (8 oz)	7–8 minutes	*Stir* or *shake* during cooking period.
Spinach, leaf or chopped	275 g (10 oz)	7–9 minutes	*Do not* add water. *Stir* or *shake* during cooking period.
Swede and Turnip, diced	225 g (8 oz)	6–7 minutes	*Stir* or *shake* during cooking period. *Mash* with butter after standing time.
Sweetcorn	225 g (8 oz)	4–6 minutes	*Stir* or *shake* during cooking period.

TIME AND SETTINGS FOR FRESH VEGETABLES

Vegetables need very little water added when microwaved. When using these charts add 30 ml (2 tbsp) water unless otherwise stated. In this way they retain their colour, flavour and nutrients more than they would if cooked conventionally. They can be cooked in boil-in-the-bags, plastic containers and polythene bags—pierce the bag before cooking to make sure there is a space for steam to escape.

Prepare vegetables in the normal way. It is most important that food is cut to an even size and stems are of the same length. Vegetables with skins, such as aubergines, need to be pierced before microwaving to prevent bursting. Season vegetables with salt after cooking if required. Salt distorts the microwave patterns and dries the vegetables.

Vegetable	Quantity	Approximate time on HIGH	Microwave Cooking Technique(s)
Artichoke, globe	1	5–6 minutes	*Place* upright in covered dish.
	2	7–8 minutes	
	3	11–12 minutes	
	4	12–13 minutes	
Asparagus	450 g (1 lb)	7–8 minutes	*Place* stalks towards the outside of the dish. *Re-position* during cooking.
Aubergine	450 g (1 lb) 0.5 cm ($\frac{1}{4}$ inch) slices	5–6 minutes	*Stir* or *shake* after 4 minutes.
Beans, broad	450 g (1 lb)	6–8 minutes	*Stir* or *shake* after 3 minutes and test after 5 minutes.
Beans, green	450 g (1 lb) sliced into 2.5 cm (1 inch) lengths	10–13 minutes	*Stir* or *shake* during the cooking period. Time will vary with age.
Beetroot, whole	4 medium	14–16 minutes	*Pierce* skin with a fork. *Re-position* during cooking.
Broccoli	450 g (1 lb) small florets	7–8 minutes	*Re-position* during cooking. *Place* stalks towards the outside of the dish.
Brussels sprouts	225 g (8 oz)	4–6 minutes	*Stir* or *shake* during cooking.
	450 g (1 lb)	7–10 minutes	
Cabbage	450 g (1 lb) quartered	8 minutes	*Stir* or *shake* during cooking.
	450 g (1 lb) shredded	8–10 minutes	
Carrots	450 g (1 lb) small whole	8–10 minutes	*Stir* or *shake* during cooking.
	450 g (1 lb) 0.5 cm ($\frac{1}{4}$ inch) slices	9–12 minutes	
Cauliflower	whole 450 g (1 lb)	9–12 minutes	*Stir* or *shake* during cooking.
	225 g (8 oz) florets	5–6 minutes	
	450 g (1 lb) florets	7–8 minutes	
Celery	450 g (1 lb) sliced into 2.5 cm (1 inch) lengths	8–10 minutes	*Stir* or *shake* during cooking.
Corn-on-the-cob	2 cobs 450 g (1 lb)	6–7 minutes	*Wrap* individually in greased greaseproof paper. *Do not* add water. *Turn* over after 3 minutes.

Courgettes	450 g (1 lb) 2.5 cm (1 inch) slices	5–7 minutes	*Do not* add more than 30 ml (2 tbsp) water. *Stir* or *shake* gently twice during cooking. *Stand* for 2 minutes before draining.
Fennel	450 g (1 lb) 0.5 cm ($\frac{1}{4}$ inch) slices	7–9 minutes	*Stir* and *shake* during cooking.
Leeks	450 g (1 lb) 2.5 cm (1 inch) slices	6–8 minutes	*Stir* or *shake* during cooking.
Mange-tout	450 g (1 lb)	7–9 minutes	*Stir* or *shake* during cooking.
Mushrooms	225 g (8 oz) whole 450 g (1 lb) whole	2–3 minutes 5 minutes	*Do not* add water. Add 25 g (1 oz) butter or alternative fat and a squeeze of lemon juice. *Stir* or *shake* gently during cooking.
Onions	225 g (8 oz) thinly sliced 450 g (1 lb) small whole	7–8 minutes 9–11 minutes	*Stir* or *shake* sliced onions. *Add only* 60 ml (4 tbsp) water to whole onions. *Re-position* whole onions during cooking.
Okra	450 g (1 lb) whole	6–8 minutes	*Stir* or *shake* during cooking.
Parsnips	450 g (1 lb) (halved)	10–16 minutes	*Place* thinner parts towards the centre. *Add* a knob of butter and 15 ml (1 tbsp) lemon juice with 150 ml ($\frac{1}{4}$ pint) water. *Turn* dish during cooking and *re-position*.
Peas	450 g (1 lb)	9–11 minutes	*Stir* or *shake* during cooking.
Potatoes			*Wash* and prick the skin with a fork.
Baked jacket	1 × 175 g (6 oz) potato 2 × 175 g (6 oz) potatoes 4 × 175 g (6 oz) potatoes	4–6 minutes 6–8 minutes 12–14 minutes	*Place* on absorbent kitchen paper or napkin. *When* cooking more than two at a time arrange in a circle. *Turn* over halfway through cooking.
Boiled (old) halved	450 g (1 lb)	7–10 minutes	*Add* 60 ml (4 tbsp) water. *Stir* or *shake* during cooking.
Boiled (new) whole	450 g (1 lb)	6–9 minutes	*Add* 60 ml (4 tbsp) water. *Do not* overcook or new potatoes become spongy.
Sweet	450 g (1 lb)	5 minutes	*Wash* and prick the skin with a fork. *Place* on absorbent kitchen paper. *Turn* over halfway through cooking time.
Spinach	450 g (1 lb) chopped	5–6 minutes	*Do not* add water. Best cooked in roasting bag, sealed with non-metal fastening. *Stir* or *shake* during cooking.
Swede	450 g (1 lb) 2 cm ($\frac{3}{4}$ inch) dice	11–13 minutes	*Stir* or *shake* during cooking.
Turnip	450 g (1 lb) 2 cm ($\frac{3}{4}$ inch) dice	9–11 minutes	*Add* 60 ml (4 tbsp) water and *stir* or *shake* during cooking.

COOKING PASTA AND RICE

Put the pasta or rice and salt to taste in a large bowl. Pour over the stated amount of boiling water. Stir and cover, leaving a gap to let steam escape, and microwave on HIGH for the stated time, stirring occasionally. Leave to stand, covered, for 5 minutes. Do not drain.

NOTE: Large quantities of pasta and rice are better cooked conventionally.

Type and quantity	Boiling water	Time on HIGH
Fresh wholemeal/spinach pasta 225 g (8 oz)	1.7 litres (3 pints)	3–4 minutes
Dried wholemeal/spinach pasta shapes 175 g (6 oz)	900 ml (1½ pints)	8–10 minutes
Dried wholemeal/spinach pasta shapes 225 g (8 oz)	900 ml (1½ pints)	8–10 minutes
Dried wholemeal/spinach pasta shapes 450 g (1 lb)	1.7 litres (3 pints)	12–14 minutes
Dried wholemeal spaghetti 225 g (8 oz)	1.1 litres (2 pints)	7–8 minutes
Dried wholemeal spaghetti 450 g (1 lb)	1.7 litres (3 pints)	8–10 minutes
Brown rice 225 g (8 oz)	450 ml (¾ pint)	30–35 minutes
White rice 225 g (8 oz)	450 ml (¾ pint)	10–12 minutes

COOKING PULSES

The following pulses will cook successfully in the microwave cooker, making considerable time savings on conventional cooking.

However, pulses with very tough skins, such as red-kidney beans, black beans, butter beans, cannellini beans, haricot beans and soya beans will not cook in less time and are better if cooked conventionally. Large quantities of all pulses are best cooked conventionally.

All pulses double in weight when cooked, so if a recipe states 225 g (8 oz) cooked beans, you will need to start with 100 g (4 oz) dried weight.

Soak beans overnight, then drain and cover with enough boiling water to come about 2.5 cm (1 inch) above the level of the beans. Cover, leaving a gap to let steam escape, and microwave on HIGH for the time stated below, stirring occasionally.

Type	Time on HIGH	
225 g (8 oz) quantity		
Aduki beans	30–35 minutes	Stand for 5 minutes
Black-eye beans	25–30 minutes	Stand for 5 minutes
Chick peas	50–55 minutes	Stand for 5 minutes
Flageolet beans	40–45 minutes	Stand for 5 minutes
Mung beans	30–35 minutes	Stand for 5 minutes
Split peas/lentils (do not need overnight soaking)	25–30 minutes	Stand for 5 minutes

Index